Happy Employees
Makes Cents

Happy Employees Makes Cents

A Roadmap for Leaders to Enrich Employee Happiness, Workplace Satisfaction and Productivity

----

Chris Huseman, Ph.D.

MAXWELL
LEADERSHIP
CERTIFIED TEAM
Independent Certified Member

ISBN: 979-8-9944761-0-9 (Hardcover)
ISBN: 979-8-9944761-1-6 (Paperback)
ISBN: 979-8-9944761-2-3 (Digital)

First Edition, 2026

Published by Huseman Leadership, LLC
Forest, Virginia

DISCLAIMER
The information in this book is for general informational and educational purposes only. The author has made every effort to ensure accuracy, but this book does not constitute professional advice. Examples and case studies may be composite representations. The author's original survey research of 386 full-time U.S. employees is described within the text. Biblical references reflect the author's interpretation and application. The author/publisher disclaims any liability arising from the use of this book's contents.

ATTRIBUTION
This book synthesizes research from numerous published sources. Every effort has been made to provide accurate citations. Survey data presented in the graphs and referenced is from the author's original research conducted in 2025. Scripture quotations are taken from the Holy Bible, New International Version®, NIV® via BibleGateway (www.biblegateway.com). Used with permission per online notice as less than 250 verses are used.

Printed in the United States of America

Website: http://www.husemanleadership.com

Author's Note and Disclaimer

I hope you find this book helpful, entertaining, thought-provoking, an instance for self-reflection, vision initiating and more. This book stands on the foundation provided by many researchers before me as well as my many years of practical experience and education. My firsthand nation-wide research has provided specific statistical insight into employee happiness, motivation, and workplace relationships with leaders among other things as they are today. I have made every attempt to cite any sources in this publication and list them at the end in the notes section, but I am human and could have missed some. If so, I am happy to make known on my website and future editions of the book any errors in this book. I used a wealth of tools to engineer this book from MS Word (no more pen and paper), spell check, auto correct, Grammarly, ChatGPT, Google, scholarly sources, professional book references, Claude AI, and more for a variety of activities from sentence structure, expanded thoughts, re-phrasing a sentence, idea generation, prompts, brainstorming, research, drafting, editing and more. Survey results were garnered and compiled using Survey Monkey. Insights were gathered by way of SPSS as well. I tip my hat in awe to those writers who wrote books before today's technologies existed. Instances and references to characters and stories are figments of possibilities inspired by a collection of past people and events I have experienced. I am in no way a health professional and nothing in this book should be considered a health prescription or mental health guidance. I am not a mental health expert and have no medical training in such. If you are experiencing mental health issues, please be strong and reach out to a licensed medical professional. Regardless, I hope this helps you towards the professional life you deserve.

Dedication

To my beautiful high school sweetheart and bride – you make me a better person. I have countless experiences I never would have had because of you. You challenge me, love me, support me through the wonderful care of our family, emulate a Christian wife and more. Thank you.

To my wonderful kids – all six of them – I love you guys. Thank you for keeping the humor in me by laughing at my horrible jokes and crazy actions and statements. I would choose each of you over and over again. I hope you each lead by creating happiness in others.

To my students – You inspire me to want to be the best I can. I hope you take up the challenge of leading this positive change opportunity into our tomorrow.

To Dr. Brian Satterlee and Dr. Tammy Brown – Thank you for your support and friendship. This book is derived in part from many of our discussions and visions of a better tomorrow. Your candor, sage advice, calmness and clarity continue to make me a better person.

To my mentors and friends, Gene Hutter, Art Ambrosi, Paul Bockewitz Sr., Ray Heilmann , Dr. Brian Satterlee and Jim Bell - your words, actions, encouragement and leadership continually have a profoundly positive influence on me.

To negative workplace experiences I have witnessed - thank you for giving me perspective on who and what not to be.

Contents

Introduction

Redefining the Business-Employee Relationship

The fundamental premise of this book rests on a simple but revolutionary idea: businesses exist to make money, and the most effective path to maximizing profitability is through happy, engaged employees. This isn't idealistic wishful thinking, it's hardheaded business strategy grounded in decades of research and validated by organizations achieving remarkable success.

Let's address the elephant in the room immediately: I'm not suggesting that the sole purpose of business is ensuring employee happiness in terms of always smiling and not having any issues. Businesses exist to create value, generate returns for investors, serve customers, and yes, make profits. Employees participate in this enterprise both to support organizational goals and to achieve their own personal objectives, financial security, professional development, meaningful contribution, personal fulfillment and more.

However, and this is the crucial insight that transforms how we think about management, it is precisely in businesses' quest to maximize profitability that they must ensure employees are as productive as possible. And research overwhelmingly demonstrates that productivity maximization happens through employee happiness and engagement, not despite it.

The False Dichotomy That's Costing Trillions

Somewhere along the way, business culture embraced a destructive myth: that employee happiness and business success represent opposing forces on a spectrum where more of one necessarily means less of the other. This zero-sum thinking has created schizophrenic organizational behaviors where executives deliver speeches about "our people being our greatest asset" on Monday, then implement policies that treat those same people as disposable expenses on Tuesday.

This false dichotomy manifests in countless ways across organizations: cutting training budgets while demanding innovation, eliminating positions while increasing workload expectations for remaining staff, implementing stack-ranking systems that pit employees against each other while praising collaboration, offering competitive salaries while creating toxic cultures that drive talent away.

The result is organizations spending enormous resources trying to optimize one side of a false equation, extracting maximum productivity from minimally engaged workers, when research clearly shows that the actual equation works entirely differently. Happy, engaged employees don't just work harder; they work smarter, innovate more, collaborate better, serve customers exceptionally, and stay with organizations longer. The productivity gains from engagement dwarf whatever efficiencies might be squeezed from disengaged workers through pressure and monitoring.

What the Research Actually Shows

This book synthesizes extensive research from organizational psychology, management science, economics, and my own primary research surveying 386 full-time U.S. employees about workplace motivation, management effectiveness, and employee satisfaction. The findings are remarkably consistent across methodologies and contexts:

Employee engagement predicts organizational performance across virtually every meaningful metric, profitability, productivity, customer satisfaction, innovation, quality, safety, and retention.

This isn't correlation mistaken for causation; studies demonstrate that improving engagement causes improved business outcomes, not merely that successful businesses happen to have engaged employees.

Gallup (2023) indicated the costs of disengagement are staggering, reaching $8.8 trillion annually in lost global productivity, roughly 9% of global GDP simply evaporating because workers are physically present but mentally absent.

The factors creating engagement are well-documented and surprisingly affordable: meaningful work, competent and supportive management, fair treatment, growth opportunities, authentic recognition, and basic human respect. Organizations don't need massive budgets to create engagement; they need competent implementation of evidence-based practices.

5

The barriers preventing organizations from creating engagement are largely systemic rather than resource-based: misaligned incentives, inadequate measurement, cultural inertia, and outdated mental models about human motivation and organizational effectiveness.

My Research: What 386 Employees Revealed

The survey research underlying this book examined full-time U.S. employees across industries, roles, and demographics to understand current workplace realities. The findings paint a sobering picture:

32.12% of workers, approximately 43 million Americans, report being motivated to do their best work only sometimes, rarely, or never. One in three workers has essentially checked out while physically showing up.

Only 22.02% of employees rate communication from management as "very good," while 30.83% rate it as poor or very poor. Management communication, one of the most fundamental leadership responsibilities, fails spectacularly across organizations.

27.72% of employees identify recognition and rewards as their primary motivator, yet 48.19% say their organization's recognition programs are ineffective, very ineffective, or nonexistent. We're failing to address a primary motivator that costs almost nothing to satisfy.

27.46% of employees, over one in four, do not trust their managers. Trust, the foundation of effective leadership, is absent for millions of workers.

These aren't abstract statistics; they represent daily workplace experiences for tens of millions of people spending the majority of their waking hours in environments that fail to engage them, recognize them, communicate with them effectively, or earn their trust.

The Business Case: Reconciling Profit with Purpose

This book makes an unabashedly capitalist argument for employee happiness. Organizations that create genuinely positive workplace experiences don't just feel good about their culture, they dramatically outperform competitors financially. Research by Gallup (2023), and other institutions consistently demonstrates that companies in the top quartile of employee engagement achieve:

- 23% higher profitability
- 14% higher productivity
- 20% higher sales
- 10% higher customer ratings
- 40% fewer quality defects
- 41% lower absenteeism
- 24-59% lower turnover (depending on industry)

These aren't marginal improvements; they're transformational advantages that compound over time. Organizations that excel at engagement don't just perform slightly better, they increasingly dominate their industries as the cumulative effects of higher productivity, lower turnover, better innovation, and superior customer service create competitive gaps that become unbridgeable.

The economic logic is straightforward: engaged employees contribute more value per hour worked, require less supervision and correction, generate more innovation, deliver better customer experiences, and stay with organizations longer. The cost of creating engagement, primarily through competent management and evidence-based practices, is modest compared to these returns. The cost of failing to create engagement, measured in turnover, lost productivity, quality issues, and missed opportunities, is astronomical.

What This Book Provides

The chapters ahead offer a comprehensive examination of workplace happiness from multiple perspectives:

The Current State: Documenting exactly how great the opportunity is, with data on disengagement levels, their causes, and their impacts on individuals and organizations.

The Research Foundation: Exploring what decades of organizational psychology, management research, and economics tell us about the relationships between employee happiness and organizational success.

The Business Case: Demonstrating through research and financial analysis that investing in employee happiness isn't just morally right, it's economically optimal.

The Responsibility Question: Examining who bears primary responsibility for employee happiness and why management holds the crucial role.

The Practical Toolkit: Providing evidence-based strategies managers can implement to foster engagement and happiness in their teams.

The Cost Analysis: Quantifying what disengagement costs organizations and society in concrete financial terms.

The Biblical Perspective: Exploring how ancient wisdom about human dignity and encouragement aligns with and reinforces modern management research.

The Barriers: Identifying what prevents well-intentioned leaders from creating happiness despite knowing its importance.

The Ripple Effects: Examining how workplace happiness or misery extends beyond organizational boundaries to affect families, communities, and society broadly.

Throughout, I maintain focus on research findings, data, and evidence-based practices rather than relying on anecdotal stories or feel-good platitudes. The goal is to provide practical, implementable guidance grounded in rigorous research for leaders who want to create both happier workplaces and better business results.

The Path Forward

We're at an inflection point in how we think about work, management, and organizational success. The old models, treating employees as costs to minimize, managing through fear and pressure, accepting disengagement as normal, are failing spectacularly. Organizations clinging to these approaches are increasingly uncompetitive against those that have discovered a better way.

The evidence is overwhelming. The practices are well-documented. The business case is compelling. The primary barrier isn't knowledge or resources; it's organizational will to acknowledge that most conventional wisdom about management and motivation is wrong and to implement what research actually shows works.

This book challenges everything many leaders think they know about work, management, and human motivation. It will make some readers uncomfortable as they recognize their own failures and the systemic dysfunction they've participated in or perpetuated. That discomfort is necessary as complacency has allowed workplace misery to become normalized when it should be seen as the organizational failure it is.

But discomfort can be productive when it motivates change. Once you see what's possible, once you understand that workplace misery isn't inevitable, that employee happiness isn't a luxury, and that human flourishing and business success are not only compatible but mutually reinforcing, the path forward becomes clear.

The research is clear. The examples are numerous. The methods are proven. The only remaining question is whether you'll have the courage to challenge conventional wisdom, the discipline to implement evidence-based practices, and the persistence to create organizations where humans thrive and businesses prosper.

The old way is dying. Organizations still treating employees as expenses, still managing through fear, still believing that happiness and profit are enemies, they're headed toward irrelevance. The future belongs to organizations that understand a fundamental truth: in an economy increasingly built on knowledge, creativity, and service, the happiness of your people isn't a nice-to-have. It's the only sustainable competitive advantage.

Welcome to a fundamentally different way of thinking about business, management, and human potential. It's time to stop accepting the false dichotomy between profit and purpose, between business success and human happiness. It's time to recognize that these aren't opposing forces but complementary elements of organizational excellence.

Let's begin.

Chapter 1

The 43 Million: When One-Third of Workers Lose Their Drive
(Are Employees Happy?)

The question seems almost quaint in its simplicity: Are employees happy? But the answer reveals a crisis that most organizations either don't see or choose to ignore. The data from my research survey of 386 full-time U.S. employees, combined with broader workplace studies, paints a troubling picture of the American workforce.

The Startling Reality: 32.12% Are Disengaged

Q4: How often do you feel motivated to do your best at work?

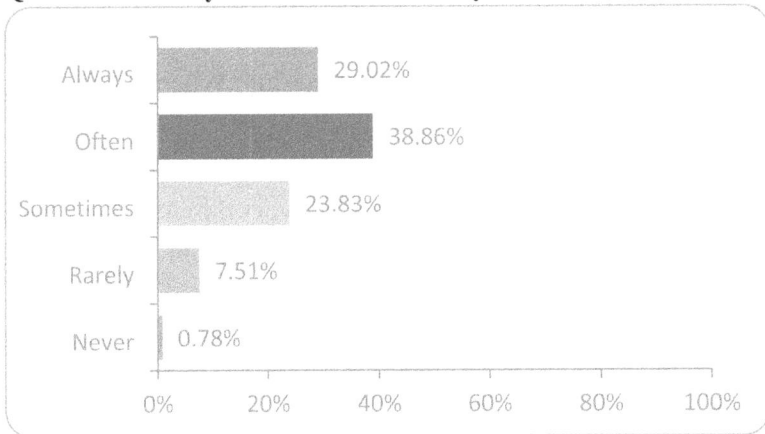

Always	29.02%
Often	38.86%
Sometimes	23.83%
Rarely	7.51%
Never	0.78%

Here's the headline finding that should alarm every business leader: 32.12% of the workforce, approximately 43,040,800 people in the United States alone, report being motivated to do their best work only sometimes, rarely, or never.

Let that sink in. One out of every three workers walking through your office doors, logging into systems, or showing up to shifts has fundamentally disconnected from their work. They're present physically but absent mentally and emotionally. They're going through the motions with all the engagement of someone performing court-ordered community service.

This isn't a small problem affecting a fringe segment. This is a mass phenomenon affecting tens of millions of workers across industries, roles, education levels, and demographics. Walk into any workplace, corporate headquarters, manufacturing floor, retail store, hospital, school, and statistically, every third person you encounter is operating on autopilot at best, actively disengaged at worst.

The economic implications are staggering. When one-third of your workforce is mentally absent, organizations are essentially running at 67% capacity on their best days. Imagine any other resource, machinery, computers, facilities, operating at two-thirds efficiency. Leaders would immediately demand solutions. Yet we've somehow normalized the same inefficiency in our most important and expensive resource: people.

According to the Bureau of Labor Statistics (BLS) the average hourly wage in the United States for full time workers is approximately $35.00 per hour. $35 per hour multiplied by 43 million people at 2,000 hours per year equates to just over $3 trillion dollars spent on workers who are not very motivated at the workplace. Chris Robinson (Drift to Drive) writes "60% of employees say they feel disengaged at work. In hard dollars, that disengagement, that lack of enthusiasm and vision and excitement comes in at a price tag of over $7.8 trillion." Regardless of what inputs you use to calculate the effect of low motivation, it is costing the economy a tremendous amount of lost value. Managers and leaders need to take advantage of this opportunity to ensure all employees realize their value and potential.

Breaking Down the 43 Million: Three Levels of Disengagement

The 32.12% who are disengaged aren't a monolithic group. My research identifies three distinct categories, each with different characteristics and implications envisioned:

The Sometimes Motivated: 23.83% of the Workforce

These workers represent the largest segment, approximately 32 million Americans. They're like smartphones at 20% battery: still functional but everyone knows they won't last long. On good days, when conditions align favorably, they can engage and contribute meaningfully. On bad days, which are increasingly frequent, they're just marking time until they can leave.

The Sometimes Motivated are particularly tragic because many still harbor hope that conditions will improve. They haven't completely given up. They still care enough to be disappointed when their contributions go unrecognized, when management makes poor decisions, or when opportunities for growth don't materialize. This residual hope makes their situation especially painful, they keep investing emotional energy in the possibility of improvement that rarely arrives.

What pushes someone into this category? Harter et al. (2020) and others point to several common patterns:

Inconsistent management attention where recognition and support appear randomly rather than systematically (Steelman et al., 2004). These employees get praised occasionally, just often enough to maintain hope, but not consistently enough to feel genuinely valued.

Exclusion from decisions affecting their work (Morrison, 2014). They have expertise and insights but aren't consulted. They see problems that leadership doesn't acknowledge. They understand what customers need but can't influence product or service design.

Workload volatility that swings between boredom and overwhelm without finding sustainable middle ground (Maslach & Leiter, 2008). Quiet periods where they question their value alternate with crisis periods where they're expected to sacrifice everything for the organization.

The Sometimes Motivated face an exhausting emotional pattern: moments of engagement followed by disappointment, brief optimism crushed by reality, effort expended without recognition. Over time, this emotional whipsaw depletes resilience and energy. Many eventually transition into the next category.

The Rarely Motivated: 7.51% of the Workforce

This segment represents approximately 10 million workers who have been burned, overlooked, or ground down so many times that hope has become a luxury they can't afford. They show up because they need the paycheck, but they've stopped expecting anything beyond compensation. They're the walking wounded of the workplace.

The Rarely Motivated aren't lazy, they've learned through repeated experience that effort doesn't correlate with reward, that excellence goes unnoticed, and that caring leads to disappointment. They've developed psychological strategies to protect themselves from further harm: emotional distance, minimum viable effort, saving passion for life outside work.

What creates Rarely Motivated employees? The patterns may be depressingly consistent:

Ideas and initiatives repeatedly ignored or dismissed. They see problems and suggest solutions, only to watch nothing change. Eventually, they stop suggesting.

Contributions that go unrecognized regardless of quality. They deliver excellent work that disappears into the organizational void without acknowledgment. They watch mediocre performers get promoted while their own exceptional performance goes unnoticed.

Promises consistently broken by management. They're told about opportunities for growth, potential promotions, or forthcoming resources that never materialize. They learn not to believe what leadership says.

What's particularly sad about the Rarely Motivated is that many were once highly engaged. They didn't start their careers checked out, they got that way through systematic organizational failure to recognize, develop, and reward their contributions. They're not the problem; they're the symptom.

These workers often create rich, fulfilling lives outside of work where they feel competent, valued, and effective. The contrast between their engaged outside-work selves and their disengaged at-work selves reveals that the problem isn't with them, it's with the workplace environment that's failed them.

The Never Motivated: 0.82% of the Workforce

This might seem like a small percentage, but we're still discussing over one million workers who have achieved complete motivational flatline. These aren't lazy people avoiding work, they're people who have emotionally divorced themselves from their jobs so completely that motivation has become irrelevant.

The Never Motivated have transcended caring. They've moved beyond disappointment or frustration into a state of profound disconnection where workplace events simply don't register emotionally. They clock in, execute required tasks with mechanical precision, and clock out without any psychological investment in outcomes.

This group often includes people who have experienced severe workplace trauma, systematic mistreatment, discrimination, harassment, betrayal of trust, that has destroyed any possibility of emotional engagement. For some, complete disconnection functions as psychological self-protection: if I don't care, I can't be hurt.

What's striking about the Never Motivated is their consistency. Unlike the Sometimes Motivated who fluctuate, these workers maintain steady low engagement regardless of external circumstances. Good news doesn't excite them. Bad news doesn't discourage them. They've achieved an almost stoic-like state of workplace detachment.

Many cycle through multiple employers while remaining in this category, having concluded that all organizations are fundamentally the same. The specific company, industry, or role matters little because their disengagement has become generalized rather than situation-specific.

The Root Causes: Why People Disengage

Understanding that millions of workers are disengaged matters less than understanding why they're disengaged. Some research points to several systemic factors that consistently predict disengagement:

Poor Management Practices

People don't quit companies; they quit managers. This truism appears in virtually every study of employee turnover and engagement. Research supports this overwhelmingly: managers account for at least 70% of the variance in employee engagement scores (Gallup, 2015), making management quality one of the strongest predictors of employee engagement.

Poor management manifests in predictable ways: micromanaging that signals distrust, providing only critical feedback while ignoring good work, making unilateral decisions without input, failing to communicate context or rationale for decisions, being inconsistently available or responsive, and setting unclear expectations while demanding accountability for outcomes (Skogstad et al., 2007; Tepper, 2000).

My research reveals troubling data about management effectiveness:

15.54% of employees say management never motivates them, approximately 20.8 million people whose managers provide zero motivational support.

38.08% rate purposeful actions by management to motivate employees as poor, very poor, or not purposeful at all. Within this group, 16.32% say management isn't purposeful in motivating them at all, roughly 22 million workers whose managers make no deliberate effort to engage them.

Management ranks as the last source of motivation for 31.87% of respondents when asked to identify what motivates them at work.

These numbers document systematic management failure at scale. We're not talking about occasional leadership mistakes but widespread, chronic inability or unwillingness to perform basic management functions like motivation, communication, and support.

Lack of Recognition

My survey data reveals that 27.72% of employees identify recognition and rewards as their primary motivator, more than one in four workers whose engagement depends substantially on feeling noticed and appreciated.

Yet here's the organizational failure found from Question 6 of my study: 48.19% of employees say their organization's recognition programs are ineffective (19.95%), very ineffective (9.59%), or nonexistent (18.65%). Nearly half of workers report that the very thing that would engage more than a quarter of them is either done poorly or not done at all.

The disconnect is stunning. Organizations know recognition matters, they conduct surveys, hire consultants, implement programs. But somehow, these efforts fail to create the experience of being genuinely recognized. Employees perceive recognition programs as box-checking exercises, political tools rewarding favorites, or generic gestures that feel manufactured rather than authentic.

The tragedy is that authentic recognition costs almost nothing: specific acknowledgment of contributions, timely feedback about good work, public or private appreciation depending on individual preferences all suffice in part. These don't require budgets, consultants, or complex systems. They require managers who pay attention and express genuine appreciation. Yet we're failing at this spectacularly.

Communication Failures

Management communication might be the most fundamental leadership responsibility, yet it's one where organizations fail most consistently. The survey data documents this failure:

Only 22.02% of employees, fewer than one in four, rate communication from management to employees as "very good."

30.83% rate management communication as poor or very poor. That's approximately 41 million people whose managers communicate with all the effectiveness of autocorrect-garbled text messages.

The remaining roughly 48% rate communication as adequate but not good, they're getting information but not in ways that build understanding, engagement, or trust.

What does poor communication look like in practice? The patterns can include:

- Silence where information is needed, creating anxiety and speculation that fills information voids with worst-case scenarios.

- Vague directives without context, leaving people uncertain about priorities, expectations, or decision rationale.
- One-way broadcasting without opportunities for questions, clarification, or feedback.
- Inconsistent messaging where different leaders say contradictory things or where stated priorities don't match observed behaviors.
- Last-minute, unexpected communications that prevent planning or preparation.

Research demonstrates that communication quality, measured by relevance, clarity, and usefulness, predicts employee outcomes more strongly than communication frequency alone (Men, 2014). Employees would rather receive less information that's clear, timely, and honest than constant updates that are vague, contradictory, or obviously incomplete.

Perceived Unfairness

Research on organizational justice, perceptions of fairness in how decisions are made, how resources are distributed, and how people are treated, demonstrates powerful effects on engagement (Colquitt et al., 2001). When employees perceive unfairness, engagement plummets regardless of other positive factors.

My survey findings include relevant data points:

25.39% of employees, more than 34 million Americans, say they cannot express their opinions without fear of it affecting their jobs. This represents a fundamental failure of psychological safety as indicated by Edmondson (1999) and procedural justice.

47.41% say they feel their contributions are valued by management only sometimes, rarely, or never. Nearly half the workforce doesn't consistently feel that management recognizes their value.

These numbers document perceptions of systematic unfairness that poison engagement. When people believe they're not heard, not valued, or that speaking up will result in retaliation, they rationally withdraw engagement as self-protection.

The Demographic Dimension: Who's Most Disengaged?

While the overall disengagement numbers are troubling, examining patterns across demographics reveals important variations that can guide interventions:

Disengagement isn't distributed equally across age groups, roles, industries, or tenure levels. Some patterns emerge from the research:

Younger workers show greater engagement variability, they're more likely to experience both high engagement and high disengagement compared to older employees who cluster more toward moderate levels (Shuck, Twyford, Reio, & Shuck, 2014). This may reflect generational differences in workplace expectations and willingness to tolerate poor management practices (Deal, Stawiski, Graves, Gentry, Weber, & Ruderman, 2013).

Employee tenure shows complex effects on engagement. While early research suggested simple patterns, recent studies find that the tenure-engagement relationship varies significantly by organizational context, industry, and individual career stage (Ng & Feldman, 2015). Employees who perceive limited growth opportunities or broken organizational promises show declining engagement regardless of tenure level (Allen, Bryant, & Vardaman, 2010).

Individual contributor roles consistently show lower engagement than management positions, reflecting differences in autonomy, decision-making authority, access to information, and ability to influence work conditions (Bailey, Madden, Alfes, & Fletcher, 2017). Hierarchical position remains one of the strongest predictors of workplace engagement across industries and organizational types (Shuck et al., 2014).The implications of these demographic patterns suggest that interventions should be targeted rather than uniform. Different populations face different barriers to engagement and need different forms of support.

The Compounding Effect: How Disengagement Spreads

One of the most concerning findings from engagement research is that disengagement is contagious. Disengaged employees don't just fail to contribute, they actively undermine engagement in others through documented mechanisms (Bakker, Demerouti, & Sanz-Vergel, 2014).

Teams develop implicit performance norms through social influence. When disengaged employees contribute minimally, others tend to match these lower standards rather than maintaining high performance (Kim & Glomb, 2014). New employees are particularly vulnerable, as they seek behavioral cues from veterans about workplace norms. Disengaged veterans effectively socialize newcomers into cynicism and minimal effort (Solinger, van Olffen, Roe, & Hofmans, 2013).

When team members disengage, engaged colleagues typically absorb additional workload to maintain output. This compensatory effort creates unsustainable burden leading to burnout, transforming today's engaged employees into tomorrow's disengaged (Bakker et al., 2014).

Emotional contagion amplifies these effects. Negative emotions, frustration, cynicism, resentment, spread from disengaged employees to colleagues through modelling, degrading team climate even for those not directly experiencing problems (Barsade & Gibson, 2012).

These mechanisms interact, creating self-reinforcing cycles where disengagement spreads throughout organizations. Conversely, improving engagement produces multiplier effects as engaged employees positively influence colleagues.

The Cost of Ignoring the 43 Million

The existence of 43 million disengaged American workers, and hundreds of millions globally, isn't just a human tragedy but an economic catastrophe. These workers can cost their organizations through:

- Lost productivity as they contribute fraction of their capability
- Increased errors requiring correction and rework
- Lower innovation as they don't propose improvements or creative solutions
- Degraded customer experiences as they go through motions without genuine care
- Higher turnover as they eventually leave for any marginally better alternative
- Poisoned team dynamics as their disengagement affects colleagues

Aggregate these individual impacts across millions of workers and you get the $9.6 trillion in annual global lost productivity that subsequent chapters will explore in detail.

But beyond economic costs, there are human costs. People spending 40-60 hours weekly in disengaged states are sacrificing enormous portions of their lives to pointless suffering. They're developing cynicism, losing confidence, and wasting potential. They're going home depleted rather than energized, affecting families and communities. They're learning that work must be endured rather than enjoyed, lessons that shape their children's expectations.

The Path Forward

Understanding that one-third of workers are disengaged is a start, but only a start. The subsequent chapters explore:

- Why engagement matters economically (Chapter 2-4)
- Who bears responsibility for fixing it (Chapter 5)

- How managers can create engagement (Chapter 6)
- What disengagement costs specifically (Chapter 7)
- What ancient wisdom adds to modern research (Chapter 8)
- Why leaders fail to fix what they know is broken (Chapter 9)
- How workplace conditions ripple beyond organizational boundaries (Chapter 10)

The 43 million disengaged American workers aren't a permanent fixture of the employment landscape. They're the predictable result of management practices that research has shown don't work. They can become engaged again, but only if organizations acknowledge the problem, understand its causes, and commit to implementing what research has proven works.

Rory Vaden, MBA CSP CPAE (Take the Stairs) reminds us "Having a Take the Stairs mind-set means that you don't just recognize your inadequacies, you resolve them. You don't just identify changes you need to make; you make them. Being a successful person requires that you take action." If you feel less motivated at work and start what Zig Ziglar of Ziglar, Inc referred to as "Stinking Thinking", we must control our thought patterns. Author Jennie Allen (Get Out of Your Head) writes "we have to remind ourselves that change is possible. We have a choice! And the more often we grab hold of that truth, the easier it will be to interrupt the downward spiral of our thoughts.".

The question isn't whether we can fix mass disengagement. **The question is whether we will**, whether the evidence will overcome inertia, whether courage will overcome comfort, and whether commitment to human flourishing will overcome acceptance of human waste.

The 43 million are waiting. What comes next depends on whether leaders choose to act on what research has been telling us for decades: **that people don't have to be miserable at work, that engagement isn't impossible or even particularly expensive, and that organizations that get this right don't just create happier humans, they build better businesses.**

Chapter 2

The Happiness Advantage: Building Profitable Organizations Through Well-Being

(Does Employee Happiness Contribute to Company Profitability?)

The previous chapter documented the scale of workplace disengagement, 43 million American workers operating at a fraction of their capability. Now comes the crucial question that every business leader must answer: Does fixing this problem actually matter financially? Or is employee happiness just a nice-to-have that we can afford only after achieving profitability?

The answer, backed by decades of research across multiple disciplines, is unequivocal: happiness doesn't just contribute to profitability, it's one of the strongest predictors of it. Organizations that create genuinely positive workplace experiences don't just feel good about their culture; they systematically and substantially outperform competitors on virtually every financial and operational metric that matters.

This chapter synthesizes research from organizational psychology, management science, economics, and business performance studies to demonstrate a truth that challenges conventional wisdom: happiness fuels success, not the other way around.

Challenging the Conventional Wisdom

The traditional business narrative runs something like this: work hard, achieve success, then you can be happy. First come the long hours, the sacrifices, the grinding effort. Success follows for those who endure. Happiness is the reward that comes after, the vacation you take after closing the deal, the satisfaction of hitting targets, the comfort that comes from financial security.

This narrative is so deeply embedded in business culture that challenging it feels almost heretical. Yet research consistently demonstrates it's backwards. The actual relationship runs in the opposite direction: happiness fuels success, not the other way around.

Shawn Achor's (2010) research, documented extensively in "The Happiness Advantage," demonstrates this through multiple studies. Positive emotions don't follow success; they precede and predict it. Happy employees don't become productive; productive employees were happy first. Engagement doesn't result from achievement; achievement results from engagement.

The mechanism works through multiple pathways that research has documented:

Cognitive and Emotional Resources: Positive emotions build psychological resources that enhance work performance. Research demonstrates that workplace happiness increases cognitive flexibility, creative problem-solving, and information processing effectiveness (Fredrickson &

Branigan, 2005). Happy employees experience broader attention spans and make more integrative decisions than stressed colleagues, enabling superior performance on complex tasks.

Energy and Persistence: Happy employees bring more energy to work and persist longer when facing challenges. The Job Demands-Resources model shows that positive emotional states create personal resources, optimism, self-efficacy, resilience, that enable sustained effort and goal pursuit even when encountering obstacles (Bakker & Demerouti, 2017). They maintain motivation through difficulties because positive emotions replenish depleted psychological resources.

Social Connection and Collaboration: Happiness facilitates relationship building, which enables collaboration, information sharing, and mutual support, all essential for complex work in modern organizations. Research demonstrates that positive affect enhances cooperative behaviors, trust development, and social bonding within teams (Kok et al., 2013).

Adaptive Behaviors: Happy employees demonstrate greater behavioral flexibility and willingness to engage with challenges. They are more likely to try new approaches, seek feedback, learn from mistakes, and adapt strategies, behaviors that drive both individual and organizational performance (Diener & Seligman, 2004). They bounce back from setbacks more quickly, maintaining productivity through challenges that would derail disengaged colleagues.

The research is clear: organizations that prioritize employee happiness create conditions for superior performance. Those that treat happiness as a reward for success have the causation backwards and pay the price in persistent underperformance.

Productivity Gains

Multiple studies examining the relationship between employee happiness and productivity find consistent results. Research published in the Journal of Labor Economics found that each one-unit increase in happiness (on a 0-10 scale) led to a 12%-13% increase in productivity (Oswald, A. J., Proto, E., & Sgroi, D., 2015).

These aren't small effects that might be measurement artifacts. They're large, consistent findings replicated across different methodologies, industries, and contexts. Happy workers don't produce slightly more, they produce substantially more.

The productivity advantage likely operates through several mechanisms. Happy workers may maintain better focus and energy throughout the day, enabling faster task completion. Positive emotions may support greater attention to quality and detail. Happy employees might waste less time on unproductive activities like complaining or office politics. They may continuously seek process improvements rather than mindlessly repeating established approaches. Research confirms that happy workers voluntarily contribute discretionary effort beyond minimum requirements (Rich, Lepine, & Crawford, 2010).

Creativity and Innovation

Research demonstrates that positive emotions facilitate creative thinking while negative emotions can constrain it, with positive mood states enhancing creative problem-solving by broadening cognitive flexibility (Davis, 2009).

When people feel happy and safe, their brains explore possibilities, make novel connections, and consider diverse perspectives. When people feel stressed or threatened, their brains narrow focus to immediate threats and proven solutions. Both states serve purposes, but innovation requires the expansive thinking that happiness enables.

The practical implications are significant. Organizations spending millions on innovation consultants and formal innovation programs often neglect the most basic prerequisite: creating workplace conditions where people feel happy and safe enough to think creatively. No amount of structured brainstorming or innovation workshops can overcome the creativity-suppressing effects of chronic workplace stress and unhappiness.

Resilience and Adaptability

Research on resilience, the capacity to bounce back from setbacks and adapt to change, shows that positive emotions are associated with greater resilience and better coping abilities (Gloria & Steinhardt, 2014). Happy workers maintain performance through challenges that cause disengaged workers to give up or burn out.

This matters enormously in modern business environments characterized by constant change, frequent setbacks, and ongoing adaptation demands. Organizations need workforces that can maintain performance despite uncertainty, learn from failures quickly, and adapt to changing circumstances without prolonged disruption.

Organizations experiencing challenging periods, recessions, competitive threats, major changes, will weather the storm better with engaged, happy workforces able to navigate challenges more successfully. They maintain productivity better, adapt faster, lose less talent, and emerge stronger. Organizations with disengaged workforces struggle, hemorrhage talent, and often don't recover.

The Social Investment: Relationships as Organizational Assets

Achor's research emphasizes that strong relationships and social support systems are crucial for both success and happiness. This creates a virtuous cycle: happiness facilitates relationship building, strong relationships support happiness, and both contribute to organizational success.

The Network Effect

Research on social networks within organizations demonstrates that relationship quality predicts performance. Teams with strong internal relationships outperform teams with weak relationships even when the latter have more talented individuals. The mechanism involves information flow, mutual support, collaborative problem-solving, and psychological safety (Edmondson, 1999).

Happy employees build stronger networks because they:

Interact more positively with colleagues, creating relationships based on genuine connection rather than transactional necessity.

Invest time in maintaining relationships rather than minimizing social interaction.

Support colleagues proactively rather than waiting to be asked.

Create positive emotional climates that make teams more enjoyable and psychologically safe.

Research tracking social networks over time shows that happiness spreads through networks. Each happy employee increases the happiness probability of nearby colleagues by approximately 15% (Fowler & Christakis, 2008). This creates multiplier effects where pockets of happiness expand throughout organizations while pockets of misery similarly spread.

Collaboration Quality

Modern organizational work increasingly requires collaboration, cross-functional teams, matrix structures, project-based work, distributed teams. Collaboration quality depends heavily on relationship quality, which depends on the emotional states people bring to interactions.

Research from Edmondson (1999) and others on team effectiveness consistently identifies psychological safety , the sense that it's safe to take interpersonal risks, ask questions, admit mistakes, and challenge ideas, as a critical factor predicting team performance. Google's Project Aristotle, which analyzed hundreds of teams to identify success factors, found psychological safety was the single most important predictor of high performance.

Psychological safety requires positive relationships built on trust, respect, and genuine care. These relationships don't develop in workplaces characterized by fear, stress, and unhappiness. They require positive emotional climates that happy employees create and sustain.

Knowledge Sharing

Knowledge-intensive work requires that people share what they know rather than hoarding information. Wang & Noe (2010) in part demonstrates that knowledge sharing depends on trust, relationship quality, and emotional climate , all factors that happiness influences.

Unhappy employees hoard knowledge because sharing requires effort and trust. Why invest time teaching colleagues if you're disengaged? Why share insights that might benefit others when you're in survival mode? Why trust that shared knowledge will be credited appropriately when you don't trust management?

Happy employees share knowledge because they have energy to invest, they trust colleagues and management, and they're oriented toward collective success rather than just personal survival. The organizational benefits of knowledge sharing are substantial, reduced duplication of effort, faster problem-solving, better decision-making, and accelerated learning.

The Business Performance Evidence

While the mechanisms explaining how happiness drives performance are interesting, what ultimately matters to business leaders is whether the effects show up in actual business results. The research on this question is extensive and the findings are remarkably consistent.

Gallup's Meta-Analysis

Gallup (2022) has conducted extensive research on employee engagement and business outcomes, analyzing data from thousands of business units across industries. Their findings, published in multiple meta-analyses, document that business units in the top quartile of employee engagement substantially outperform those in the bottom quartile:

- 21% higher profitability
- 17% higher productivity
- 20% higher sales
- 10% higher customer ratings
- 40% fewer quality defects
- 41% lower absenteeism
- 24-59% lower turnover (depending on industry)

These aren't marginal differences, they're transformational advantages that compound over time. Organizations achieving top-quartile engagement don't just perform slightly better; they increasingly dominate their markets as cumulative advantages create widening performance gaps.

Stock Market Performance

Research examining stock performance of companies recognized as excellent workplaces demonstrates significant market outperformance, with Fortune's '100 Best Companies to Work For' generating substantial abnormal returns compared to market indexes (Edmans, 2011, 2012).

This premium reflects multiple factors: lower turnover saves costs, higher productivity improves margins, better innovation drives growth, superior customer service protects market share, and employer brand attracts better talent. All of these factors flow from the workplace conditions that earn "best place to work" recognition, conditions that create employee happiness and engagement.

Industry-Specific Studies

Research across industries confirms the happiness-performance relationship.

Retail stores with engaged employees achieve higher sales and customer satisfaction through better service and lower turnover (Harter, Schmidt, & Hayes, 2002).

Healthcare facilities with engaged staff demonstrate better patient outcomes, fewer medical errors, and higher patient satisfaction, as happy healthcare workers provide more attentive care and maintain focus during demanding shifts (Laschinger & Leiter, 2006).

Manufacturing plants with engaged workforces achieve higher productivity, better quality, fewer safety incidents, and less downtime through greater attention, proactive problem-solving, and better equipment maintenance (Harter et al., 2020).

The pattern holds across industries: engagement predicts performance whether organizations sell products, provide services, manufacture goods, or develop software.

The ROI of Happiness Investments

Perhaps the most compelling business case for employee happiness comes from examining the return on investment of initiatives that improve workplace conditions.

Intervention Studies

Research examining engagement interventions demonstrates measurable organizational improvements. A systematic review and meta-analysis of workplace engagement interventions found that well-designed programs effectively increase employee engagement, with positive effects on wellbeing and performance outcomes (Knight, Patterson, & Dawson, 2017). Intervention effectiveness depends on implementation quality, organizational support, and sustained commitment rather than simply adopting programmatic solutions.

The costs of engagement initiatives are typically modest compared to potential returns. Most interventions focus on improving management practices, implementing recognition systems, enhancing communication, and creating development opportunities, changes requiring primarily training and process adjustments rather than substantial capital investments (Schneider, Macey, Barbera, & Martin, 2009).

Cost Avoidance

Beyond direct performance improvements, engagement initiatives generate returns through cost avoidance. Research on employee turnover demonstrates that replacing employees costs 50-200% of annual salary depending on role complexity, making retention improvements from engagement initiatives particularly valuable financially (Allen, Bryant, & Vardaman, 2010). Organizations improving engagement experience reduced turnover, lower absenteeism, fewer quality problems, reduced safety incidents, lower healthcare costs, and decreased recruiting expenses.

Competitive Advantage

Workplace happiness creates sustainable competitive advantages that competitors struggle to replicate. Research demonstrates that hard-to-imitate human resource practices, including those fostering engagement, provide sustained competitive advantage because they're socially complex, causally ambiguous, and deeply embedded in organizational culture (Wright, Dunford, & Snell, 2001). Strong employer brands attract superior talent, retention preserves institutional knowledge, engaged cultures drive continuous innovation, and operational advantages compound over time, creating widening performance gaps between engaged and disengaged organizations.

These advantages create widening gaps between high-engagement and low-engagement competitors. Initially small performance differences compound into dominant market positions that become increasingly difficult to challenge.

Achor's Challenge to Management

Shawn Achor's (2010) research culminates in a direct challenge to management: prioritize employee happiness not as a nice-to-have but as a strategic imperative. His argument, supported by extensive research, is that positive workplace culture leads to higher productivity, better performance, and greater overall success.

This challenges the traditional management mindset in several fundamental ways:

Happiness as Input, Not Output

Traditional thinking treats happiness as an output, something that results from success. Achor's research demonstrates it's an input, something that enables success. This reversal has profound implications for management priorities and resource allocation.

If happiness is output, you focus on driving performance and assume happiness follows. If happiness is input, you focus on creating conditions for happiness and performance follows. The evidence clearly supports the latter.

Investment vs. Expense

Traditional thinking treats employee wellbeing as an expense, nice to have when affordable but expendable when budgets tighten. Achor's research demonstrates it's an investment, something that generates returns exceeding costs.

This reframing has significant implications for how organizations approach workplace improvements. Expenses get cut when times are tough. Investments get protected because they generate returns. Treating happiness as investment rather than expense changes decision-making fundamentally.

Leading vs. Lagging Indicators

Traditional management focuses on lagging indicators, financial results, productivity metrics, quality measures. These tell you how you performed but not how you'll perform tomorrow. Achor's research suggests treating happiness and engagement as leading indicators, factors that predict future performance.

Organizations that monitor engagement as carefully as they monitor financial results can identify problems before they show up in business metrics. They can intervene proactively rather than reactively. They can manage the drivers of performance rather than just measuring outcomes.

The Uncomfortable Truth

Here's what makes Achor's challenge uncomfortable for many leaders: accepting it requires admitting that conventional management wisdom is wrong. It requires acknowledging that decades of management practice have had the causation backwards, that organizations have sacrificed enormous value by treating happiness as a luxury rather than a necessity.

This is difficult to accept because it implies that management bears responsibility for underperformance that could have been avoided. It suggests that low engagement isn't an unfortunate reality to be accepted but a failure to be fixed. It means that the "tough" managers who drove results through pressure and fear were actually destroying value, not creating it. I have experienced this first hand many times where a great group of employees continually searched for another job simply because they were tired of the managers who controlled them with fear and harshness.

But discomfort doesn't make research wrong. The evidence is overwhelming, the mechanisms are well-understood, and the financial benefits are clearly documented. The question isn't whether happiness drives performance, decades of research confirm it does. The question is whether leaders will have the courage to act on what research tells us despite how uncomfortable it makes them.

Conclusion: The Happiness Imperative

Employee happiness isn't a distraction from business success, it's a prerequisite for it. Organizations that create genuinely positive workplace experiences don't sacrifice performance for feel-good culture; they achieve superior performance through culture that enables human flourishing. The research such as from Achor (2010) and others is unambiguous:

- Happiness predicts productivity, not vice versa
- Positive emotions enhance creativity, problem-solving, and resilience
- Strong relationships enable collaboration and knowledge sharing
- Engaged organizations outperform disengaged competitors across all meaningful metrics
- Investments in happiness generate substantial, measurable returns

The traditional business narrative, that success leads to happiness, is backwards. Happiness leads to success. Organizations that understand this and act accordingly create competitive advantages that compound over time. Those that cling to outdated models sacrifice enormous value while wondering why competitors keep pulling ahead.

The happiness advantage is real, measurable, and available to any organization willing to prioritize what research has proven matters. The only question is whether leaders will have the wisdom to recognize this truth and the courage to act on it.

Chapter 3

The 13% Advantage: How Happy Employees Drive Business Success
(Do Employees Need to Be Happy at Work to Be Productive?)

The previous chapter established that employee happiness contributes to profitability. This chapter examines a more fundamental question: Is happiness actually necessary for productivity, or can organizations achieve results through other means, pressure, incentives, careful monitoring, or sheer force of will?

The research answer is clear and might surprise those raised on traditional management thinking: yes, employees need to be happy at work to achieve optimal productivity. I'm not talking about just "nice to have" happiness that makes everyone feel good, but genuine satisfaction and engagement that research demonstrates is essential for sustainable high performance.

This isn't soft thinking or naive idealism. It's hardheaded recognition of how human psychology, motivation, and cognitive function actually work. Organizations that ignore the happiness-productivity link don't just create miserable workplaces, they systematically underperform their potential while competitors who understand this relationship pull ahead.

The Voice Crisis: 25% Can't Speak Freely

Have you ever been told to quit asking difficult questions at work? Have you ever been threatened with a note to be placed in your personnel file for taking initiative? My survey research revealed a troubling finding that undermines productivity in profound ways: 25.39% of employees, more than 34 million American workers, say they cannot express their opinions without fear of it affecting their jobs negatively.

Think about what this means operationally. More than one in four workers believes that speaking up, sharing concerns, identifying problems, suggesting improvements, asking clarifying questions, or challenging flawed thinking, will result in personal consequences. So, they stay silent even when they see problems, know better approaches, or recognize risks that leadership is missing.

Q8: Are you able to express your opinion to management without fear of it affecting your job status?

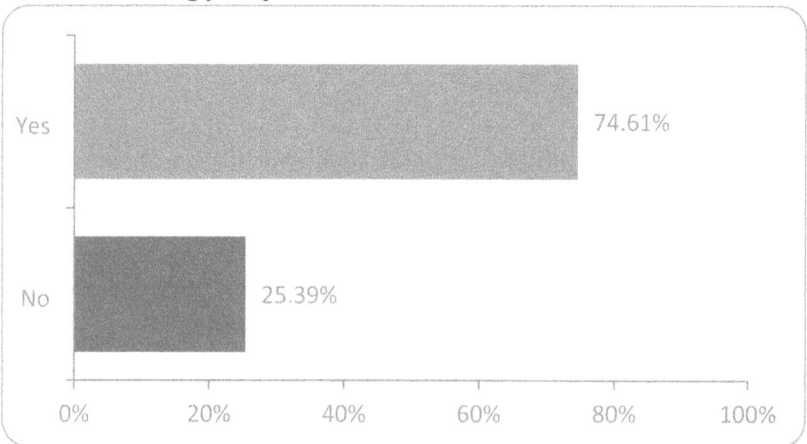

Yes — 74.61%
No — 25.39%

With nearly 75% indicating "Yes", we have a lot of leaders that are doing a great job in listening to employees! Adam Grant (Originals) writes, "When it comes to the powerful ideas in our heads and the core values in our hearts, we censor ourselves. 'There are so few originals in life,' says renowned executive Mellody Hobson, 'because people are afraid to speak up and stand out.'" John P. Kotter (Leading Change) discusses the old "command-and-control" style of leadership that "snuffs out initiative and creativity as quickly as carbon dioxide kills a fire". Part of Kotter's solution is honest dialogue as "discouraged and disempowered employees never make enterprises winners…" Simon Sinek (Leaders Eat Last) discusses how a humble leader distributes power to employees rather than use the "command-and-control" style which allows the leader to focus on training, building and protecting their employees.

Dave Ramsey (Entreleadership) writes if you want your team to buy into your dream "you must be caught caring about them personally and treating them with dignity". Part of that care is hearing ideas, critical feedback, and having that honest dialogue on a continual basis. Ron Friedman, Ph.D. (The Best Place to Work) suggests by shifting meetings (or I would add regular feedback) from what's missing to what's been achieved, taps into evidence "that the experience of progress is the single most important component of a satisfying workday". Leaders have the ability to progress employee happiness through purposeful, open and continuous dialogue that is free of fear to express their opinion.

The productivity cost of this enforced silence is enormous:

Problems Go Unreported: Employees who see safety issues, quality problems, process inefficiencies, or emerging risks stay quiet because speaking up feels dangerous. Problems that could be caught early and fixed cheaply instead escalate until they become expensive crises.

Innovation Dies: Employees with ideas for improvements, new products, better processes, or competitive advantages don't share them because the personal risk exceeds any potential reward. Innovation requires psychological safety (Edmondson, 1999) to explore untested ideas, precisely what 25% of workers lack.

Errors Multiply: When people fear admitting mistakes, errors don't get corrected quickly. They get hidden, worked around, or passed along until they cause much larger problems. Organizations that punish mistake acknowledgment guarantee that small errors become catastrophic failures.

Knowledge Stays Trapped: Employees who know things that would benefit colleagues or the organization don't share their knowledge because they're in self-protection mode. Why invest effort teaching others when you're just trying to survive?

Research on psychological safety demonstrates that teams and organizations where people feel safe speaking up dramatically outperform those where fear suppresses voice (Edmondson, 1999; Edmondson & Lei, 2014). The mechanism is straightforward: problems get identified and solved earlier, innovations get surfaced and tested, errors get corrected quickly, and knowledge flows freely."

The 25% who can't speak freely aren't just personally miserable, they represent massive organizational inefficiency. Their knowledge, insights, and observations remain locked away, unavailable to improve organizational performance. Organizations are paying these people for their expertise and judgment, then creating conditions that prevent accessing either.

The Global Quiet Quitting Crisis

Research by Gallup documenting global workplace trends reveals a phenomenon that makes the productivity-happiness connection undeniable: 50% of the global workforce is "quiet quitting", doing the minimum required but nothing more, and an additional 18% are "loud quitting," openly expressing their unhappiness and actively undermining organizational success. (Gallup, 2022)

That means roughly two-thirds of workers globally are either checked out or actively hostile. Only about one-third are genuinely engaged and willing to contribute discretionary effort. Organizations are essentially operating at one-third of their human capital potential.

Quiet Quitting: The term may be new, but the phenomenon isn't. Quiet quitters do exactly what's required to avoid negative consequences but nothing beyond that. They:

Don't volunteer for projects or initiatives
Don't stay late when crises emerge
Don't propose improvements or innovations
Don't help colleagues beyond minimum requirements
Don't invest in skill development or learning
Don't build relationships beyond transactional necessity

The productivity cost of quiet quitting is substantial. Organizations built on people doing just enough to avoid getting fired inevitably underperform organizations where people voluntarily contribute beyond requirements. Innovation, excellence, and competitive advantage don't come from minimum viable effort, they come from discretionary contribution that quiet quitters withhold.

Loud Quitting: Even more damaging than quiet quitting is the 18% who are actively disengaged, not just checked out but actively working against organizational success. These employees:

- Spread negativity that infects colleagues
- Undermine leadership initiatives
- Create conflict and drama that drains team energy
- Resist changes and improvements
- Poison new hires with cynicism
- Create quality problems through inattention or sabotage

Actively disengaged employees don't just fail to contribute, they actively subtract value from what engaged colleagues create.

The Shifted Perspective: Gallup's research notes that for many workers, perspective has shifted "from what we do for a living to how we want to live." This reflects a fundamental reassessment of work's role in life, accelerated by pandemic-era remote work and broader cultural changes. (Gallup, 2022)

Workers increasingly refuse to sacrifice their lives for jobs that don't provide meaning, respect, or genuine satisfaction. They're questioning why they should give more than minimum effort to organizations that treat them as disposable resources. This shift isn't laziness or entitlement, it's a rational response to decades of organizations extracting maximum value while providing minimum support.

Organizations can respond to this shift in two ways: fight it by trying to force people back into old patterns, or adapt by creating conditions where people want to contribute beyond minimum requirements. Research suggests the former fails while the latter succeeds.

The MIT Health and Happiness Research

Research from MIT (MIT Sloan School, 2023)'s Sloan School of Management makes an important finding: employee health and happiness at work isn't an afterthought or luxury, it's a driving force in decisions to take jobs, stay at jobs, or leave jobs. This fundamentally challenges the traditional assumption that compensation and benefits are primary drivers of employment decisions.

Research documents that when people evaluate job opportunities or consider whether to stay or leave, workplace happiness and its impact on overall wellbeing rank as high as or higher than compensation in importance (Judge et al., 2010; Kahneman & Deaton, 2010). People will accept lower pay for work that makes them genuinely happy (Burbano, 2016). They'll reject higher pay for work that makes them miserable (Griffeth et al., 2000).

This has profound implications for productivity. Organizations that create unhappy workplaces face three related problems:

Selection Problems: They attract people for whom compensation matters more than happiness, often those with limited options or significant financial pressures. These aren't necessarily bad employees, but they're not joining because they're excited about the work or committed to the mission. They're joining despite reservations because they need the money.

Retention Problems: Good employees leave as soon as better options emerge. Organizations that make people unhappy become stepping stones rather than destinations, places people work while actively seeking alternatives. This creates constant turnover that disrupts productivity, destroys institutional knowledge, and requires endless recruiting and training.

Motivation Problems: Employees who are at jobs primarily for compensation rather than satisfaction are inherently less motivated to contribute beyond minimum requirements. They're doing a transaction, time and minimum effort for money, rather than investing themselves in meaningful work.

The MIT research suggests that organizations creating genuinely positive workplace experiences solve all three problems simultaneously. They attract people who want to be there, retain people who continue choosing to stay despite other options, and motivate people to contribute beyond transactional requirements. The productivity advantages compound across all three dimensions.

The Oxford Causal Link: 13% Productivity Increase

While many studies document correlations between happiness and productivity, research from Oxford University's Saïd Business School established something more powerful: a causal link demonstrating that happiness directly causes productivity increases (University of Oxford, Saïd Business School, 2023).

The study, conducted over multiple years with rigorous controls, found that happy workers are 13% more productive than unhappy workers performing identical tasks. This isn't correlation that might be explained by other factors, it's demonstrated causation showing that happiness itself drives productivity gains.

The 13% figure is worth emphasizing because it's so substantial. In most industries, productivity improvements of 2-3% are considered significant achievements worth major investment. A 13% improvement is transformational, it's the difference between industry leadership and mediocrity, between healthy margins and barely breaking even, between sustainable growth and stagnant performance.

The implications are profound. If happiness alone produces a 13% productivity increase, it becomes one of the highest-ROI investments organizations can make. Most productivity improvement initiatives, new technology, process optimization, training programs, cost substantial amounts and deliver single-digit percentage improvements. Creating workplace happiness costs relatively little and delivers double-digit productivity gains.

The Meaning Connection: Pew Research Findings

Pew Research Center (2021)'s studies on meaning in life reveal that work ranks second only to family and children as a source of life meaning for most people. This finding is crucial for understanding the productivity-happiness connection.

When work provides meaning, when people feel their efforts matter, contribute to something important, and align with their values, they experience higher job satisfaction, stronger engagement, and deeper organizational commitment. When work feels meaningless, when people see their efforts as pointless, contributing to nothing important, or contradicting their values, satisfaction plummets, engagement disappears, and commitment evaporates.

The productivity implications flow directly from this meaning connection:

Intrinsic Motivation: Meaningful work generates intrinsic motivation, people work hard because the work itself is rewarding. Meaningless work requires extrinsic motivation, people need external pressure or rewards to maintain effort. Research consistently shows intrinsic motivation produces better sustained performance.

Discretionary Effort: People doing meaningful work voluntarily contribute beyond requirements. People doing meaningless work contribute exactly what's required and not a bit more. The productivity differential between discretionary contribution and minimum viable effort is substantial. Ever stay late at work because you wanted to?

Resilience Through Challenges: Meaningful work sustains motivation through difficulties. When work matters, people persist through obstacles, setbacks, and frustrations. Meaningless work lacks this sustaining power, why persist through difficulty when the destination doesn't matter?

Identity and Pride: Meaningful work becomes part of identity and generates pride. People tell others about work they're proud of, bringing their full selves to it, and maintaining standards even when nobody's watching. Meaningless work remains separate from identity and generates no pride, with predictable effects on quality and effort. My Optimist Club friends are perfect examples.

Organizations that help employees connect their work to meaningful outcomes, showing how their efforts help customers, improve lives, solve important problems, or contribute to valued goals, create the conditions for happiness and the productivity that flows from it. Those that treat work as purely transactional and never connect tasks to meaning sacrifice this powerful source of motivation.

The Integration: Why Happiness Is Necessary, Not Optional

Happy Employees bring many benefits as I have tried to demonstrate so far:

Cognitive Function: Happy brains work better, they're more creative, solve problems more effectively, maintain focus longer, and make better decisions. Unhappy brains operate in survival mode, narrowing attention and defaulting to safe, proven approaches even when innovation is needed.

Motivation: Happy employees are intrinsically motivated, contributing discretionary effort beyond requirements. Unhappy employees need constant external motivation, contributing only what's required to avoid consequences.

Learning and Adaptation: Happy employees embrace learning and change. Unhappy employees resist both because they require energy and optimism that unhappiness depletes.

Collaboration: Happy employees build relationships, share knowledge, and support colleagues. Unhappy employees isolate, hoard information, and focus on personal survival.

Persistence: Happy employees persist through challenges and setbacks. Unhappy employees give up when difficulties arise because they lack motivation to overcome obstacles.

Quality Focus: Happy employees take pride in work quality. Unhappy employees do just enough to avoid criticism.

Voice and Initiative: Happy employees speak up about problems and opportunities. Unhappy employees, particularly the 25% who fear consequences for speaking up, stay silent even when they see problems or opportunities.

Each of these factors affects productivity independently. Combined, they create enormous productivity differentials between happy and unhappy workforces.

The Uncomfortable Truth for Traditional Management

This research poses a fundamental challenge to traditional management thinking that assumes productivity can be driven through pressure, monitoring, and consequences. That approach might extract compliance, but research demonstrates it cannot achieve optimal productivity.

Maximum productivity requires positive emotions, intrinsic motivation, psychological safety (Edmondson, 1999), meaningful connection to work, and energy to contribute beyond minimum requirements. These cannot be forced through pressure, they can only be created through workplace conditions that generate genuine happiness and engagement.

Organizations that continue trying to drive productivity through traditional means, pressure, surveillance, consequences for insufficient output, are leaving enormous value on the table. They're achieving 70-80% of the productivity they could achieve if they created conditions for happiness. Their competitors who understand this relationship are pulling ahead by 15-25% on productivity alone, before considering other advantages like lower turnover and better innovation.

Conclusion: The Necessity of Happiness

Do employees need to be happy at work to be productive? The research answer is unambiguous: yes, if you want optimal productivity rather than minimum viable output. Happy workers aren't just more pleasant to manage, they're 12-13% more productive, more creative, more collaborative, more persistent, and more committed to quality.

Organizations can achieve some level of productivity without happiness through pressure, monitoring, and consequences. But they'll systematically underperform their potential and their competitors who create genuine workplace happiness. The productivity gap isn't small or uncertain, it's large, well-documented, and decisive.

The question isn't whether happiness matters for productivity, decades of research confirm it does. The question is whether organizations will act on this knowledge or continue pursuing outdated approaches that research has proven inferior. The answer to that question will determine which organizations thrive and which struggle in increasingly competitive environments where human capital advantages become determinative.

Chapter 4

The Business Case Revolution: Reconciling Profit with Purpose
(If Employee Happiness Contributes to Productivity, Shouldn't Companies Strive to Make Their Employees Happy?)

The previous chapters have established through research that employee happiness drives productivity and profitability. A logical conclusion follows: organizations should systematically invest in creating employee happiness as a core business strategy. Yet despite overwhelming evidence, most organizations continue treating employee wellbeing as a secondary concern, an expense to minimize, or a luxury affordable only after achieving profitability.

This chapter examines why this disconnect persists and explores how to reconcile the apparent tension between maximizing profit and maximizing employee happiness. The resolution lies in recognizing that this tension is false, that profit maximization and employee happiness aren't opposing objectives but complementary strategies that reinforce each other.

The Historical Context: Business Purpose Through Economic Theory

To understand why organizations struggle to prioritize employee happiness despite evidence of its business value, I want to examine some of the intellectual foundations that have shaped business thinking for centuries.

Adam Smith and The Wealth of Nations (1776)

Adam Smith's "The Wealth of Nations" (1776/2023) established the foundational premise of modern capitalism: that the purpose of business is to generate profit and increase wealth. Smith argued that individuals pursuing their own economic self-interest, guided by an "invisible hand," would collectively produce optimal outcomes for society.

This framework positioned profit-seeking as not just acceptable but beneficial, the mechanism through which resources get allocated efficiently and societal wealth increases. Business exists to make money, and society benefits when businesses succeed at this objective.

Smith's framework wasn't wrong, but it has been interpreted in ways that create unnecessary conflicts. The pursuit of profit doesn't require sacrificing employee wellbeing, in fact, as research demonstrates, it requires investing in it. But generations of business leaders have interpreted profit maximization as requiring cost minimization, including minimizing investment in employees beyond what's absolutely necessary. Perhaps these business leaders failed to read Smith's The Theory of Moral Sentiments as well and as such they don't have the foundation provided by Smith.

The Friedman Doctrine: Shareholder Primacy

In 1970, economist Milton Friedman published an influential essay arguing that the social responsibility of business is to increase profits. The "Friedman doctrine," also called shareholder theory, holds that corporate executives are agents of shareholders and have a duty to maximize shareholder returns.

Friedman explicitly rejected the idea that businesses have broader social responsibilities: "There is one and only one social responsibility of business, to use its resources and engage in activities designed to increase its profits so long as it stays within the rules of the game."

This doctrine has profoundly influenced business practice and management education for decades. It perhaps created intellectual justification for treating all stakeholders other than shareholders, including employees, as means to the end of profit rather than as having legitimate claims on corporate resources or consideration.

The Friedman doctrine reinforces the false dichotomy between profit and employee wellbeing. If the sole responsibility is maximizing shareholder return, any investment in employees beyond the minimum necessary becomes philosophically questionable. Employee happiness becomes at best a means to profit and at worst a distraction from it.

Profit Maximization Theory

Profit maximization theory, dominant in economics and finance, assumes the goal of a company is to make the highest profits possible. This seems straightforward and unobjectionable, of course businesses should seek to maximize profits.

The problem lies in how "profit maximization" gets interpreted in practice. Short-term profit maximization often conflicts with long-term value creation. Quarterly earnings pressure leads to decisions that boost immediate results while undermining future performance. Cost-cutting that increases current profits while destroying organizational capability and employee engagement sacrifices sustainable value for temporary gains. Fire today, hire next quarter.

Research on profit maximization demonstrates that companies focused exclusively on short-term profit maximization often underperform those balancing profit with other objectives like customer satisfaction, innovation, and employee development. The myopic pursuit of maximum quarterly profits paradoxically undermines long-term profitability.

The Profit Motive

The profit motive, the intent to achieve monetary gain, is a powerful driver of economic activity and innovation. Organizations and individuals motivated by profit create products, services, and solutions that customers value enough to pay for.

The profit motive becomes problematic only when divorced from other considerations. Pursuing profit through creating genuine value, solving real problems, meeting authentic needs, improving lives, aligns profit with social benefit.

Pursuing profit through exploitation, manipulation, or cost-shifting, paying poverty wages while others earn millions, creating products that harm while marketing benefits, polluting while externalizing cleanup costs, creates profits that come at society's expense.

Employee happiness fits naturally within a properly conceived profit motive. Happy employees create more value, generate better results, and contribute to sustainable profitability. Pursuing profit through employee engagement aligns business success with human flourishing. Pursuing profit despite employee misery may achieve short-term gains but sacrifices long-term sustainability.

The Survey Data: Employees Feel Undervalued

My research survey reveals exactly how this theoretical tension manifests in employee experience. The data documents systematic organizational failure to make employees feel valued:

47.41% Feel Contributions Aren't Consistently Valued

When asked how often they feel their contributions are valued by management, 47.41% of employees responded "sometimes," "rarely," or "never." That's nearly 64 million American workers who don't consistently feel that management recognizes or appreciates their contributions.

Breaking this down further reveals the depth of the problem:
- A substantial percentage feel valued only "sometimes", not never, but not consistently

- 13.47% feel valued "rarely"
- Nearly 9% feel valued "never"

These aren't employees demanding constant praise. They're asking for basic recognition that their work matters and their efforts are noticed. The failure to provide this fundamental human need represents organizational dysfunction at scale.

The cost of this failure extends beyond morale. Employees who don't feel valued don't go the extra mile. They don't volunteer for difficult projects. They don't take initiative to solve problems. They don't innovate. They calibrate their effort to match perceived appreciation, and when appreciation is minimal or absent, effort follows suit.

Q5: How often do you feel that your contributions are valued by your management?

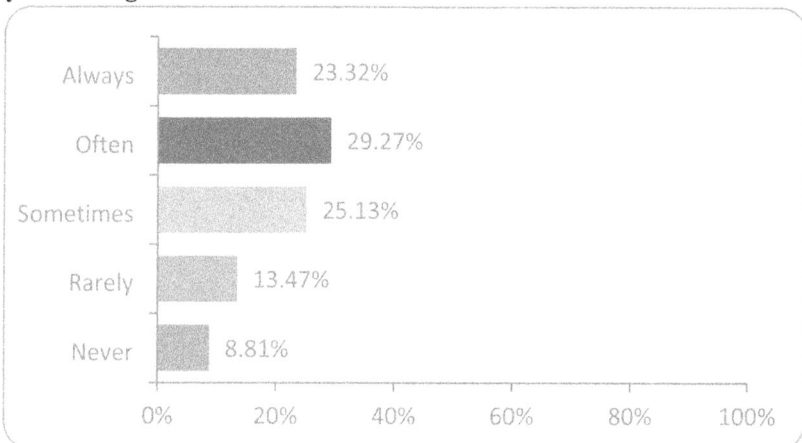

Always	23.32%
Often	29.27%
Sometimes	25.13%
Rarely	13.47%
Never	8.81%

Will Guidara (Unreasonable Hospitality, 2022) writes "The first time someone comes to you with an idea, listen closely, because how you handle it will dictate how they choose to contribute in the future" (p. 116). How many of us have experienced a negative response too often? Again, just over half the respondents indicated they felt management valued their contributions. This, again, is a very positive story that many leaders should pat themselves on the back for! Thank you leaders! But the 47.41% of the respondents, or nearly 64,000,000 full time workers, have a less than ideal perspective on management's value of their contributions. Chris Robinson (Drift to Drive, 2025) writes "...a healthy community should feel safe. But it should also feel like a safe place to fail. A safe place to hear tough feedback. A safe place to try things and see how they land" (p. 131). Chris continues "Generosity, collaboration, cheering for each other, sharing the truth compassionately - those are the marks of a healthy environment" (p.136).

If you are only getting feedback once a year in a formal manner, ask for more frequent feedback. If you and your team are only meeting once every two years, take the initiative and meet with your team members yourself. There is power in community at work. We can validate our colleagues' contributions whether through praise, challenge or critique when we do it with genuine care for them.

Tom William (T.W.) Lewis (Solid Ground, 2020) of T.W. Lewis Company and T.W. Lewis Foundation writes "As human beings, we can never flourish by just focusing on ourselves. Helping others leads to a richer, deeper and more meaningful life" (p.171).

The Recognition Gap

As documented in Chapter 1, 27.72% of employees identify recognition and rewards as their primary motivator. Yet 48.19% say their organization's recognition programs are ineffective, very ineffective, or nonexistent.

This gap reveals organizational priorities starkly. Companies invest enormous resources in systems, technology, facilities, and equipment. They'll spend millions on enterprise software or office renovations. But they fail at the comparatively inexpensive task of making people feel valued.

The disconnect suggests that despite rhetoric about "people being our greatest asset," organizations don't actually prioritize employee satisfaction. They optimize for things that are easy to measure and justify financially, ROI calculations on technology purchases, while neglecting things that are harder to quantify but more impactful on performance.

Reconciling Profit with Employee Happiness

The perceived tension between profit maximization and employee happiness might rest on several faulty assumptions that research contradicts:

Faulty Assumption 1: Employee Happiness Is Expensive

Many leaders assume creating employee happiness requires expensive perks, high compensation, generous benefits, or costly programs. The research shows this is false.

While competitive compensation matters, poverty wages create misery no amount of recognition can overcome, genuine employee happiness depends primarily on factors that cost little:

- Competent, supportive management (training investment, not ongoing cost)
- Authentic recognition (costs essentially nothing)
- Clear communication (requires discipline, not budget)
- Fair treatment (requires integrity, not resources)
- Opportunities to contribute meaningfully (requires thoughtful work design, not money)
- Psychological safety (requires culture change, not capital investment)

Organizations spending millions on perks while maintaining toxic cultures discover that ping-pong tables don't create happiness. Organizations with modest budgets but excellent management create genuinely engaged workforces. The research is clear: happiness depends more on how people are treated than on how much they're paid or what amenities are provided.

Faulty Assumption 2: Happy Employees Are Less Driven

Some leaders fear that making employees too happy will reduce their drive and performance. This assumes happiness equals complacency, that people need to be dissatisfied to be motivated.

Research thoroughly debunks this assumption. Happy employees are more productive, not less. They contribute more discretionary effort, not less. They set higher standards for themselves, not lower ones. They persist through challenges rather than giving up.

The confusion stems from conflating happiness with comfort. Making people comfortable in underperformance does create complacency. But genuine happiness at work, deriving from meaningful contribution, growth, achievement, and recognition, drives higher performance, not lower.

Organizations that create genuine engagement discover that people want to excel. They want to contribute to something meaningful. They want to grow and develop capabilities. They want to be part of successful teams. Happiness doesn't diminish these drives, it enables them by providing the psychological resources and positive emotions that fuel sustained high performance.

Faulty Assumption 3: Short-Term Profit Requires Sacrificing Employee Happiness

This assumption holds that making quarterly numbers requires decisions that hurt employees, cutting positions, reducing benefits, increasing workloads, freezing development. If forced to choose between short-term profits and employee happiness, profit must win.

Research suggests this is a false choice created by poor planning and management. Organizations that maintain employee engagement through difficult periods discover they perform better, not worse (Bakker & Demerouti, 2008):

- Engaged employees maintain productivity even when resources are constrained
- Engaged employees find creative solutions to do more with less
- Engaged employees don't abandon ship at the first sign of trouble
- Engaged employees understand that temporary challenges differ from permanent dysfunction

Organizations that sacrifice employee happiness for short-term profits discover the strategy backfires. Best performers leave, taking relationships and knowledge. Remaining employees disengage, reducing productivity. Quality suffers. Customer satisfaction declines. The short-term profit gains evaporate as these consequences compound.

Research indicates that organizations maintaining employee engagement during challenging periods outperform those that sacrifice engagement for short-term financial protection, as sustained engagement is strongly associated with higher profitability, productivity, and organizational resilience (Gallup, 2020).

Faulty Assumption 4: Shareholder Interests Conflict With Employee Interests

The Friedman doctrine assumes that what's good for shareholders (maximum profit) conflicts with what's good for employees (good treatment, fair compensation, development opportunities) rationalizing if resources go to employees, less goes to shareholders.

Contrary to zero-sum assumptions, empirical research demonstrates that employee engagement and shareholder value are complementary rather than competing objectives. Longitudinal studies show that organizations recognized as top workplaces significantly outperform market averages, while firms in the top quartile of employee engagement achieve approximately 21% higher profitability (Gallup, 2020; Fortune, 2019). Additional research finds a strong positive relationship between employee satisfaction and long-term shareholder returns (Edmans, 2011).

The mechanism is straightforward: engaged employees create more value. They're more productive, more innovative, provide better customer service, stay longer, and require less management overhead. This value creation flows to multiple stakeholders, including shareholders.

The interests of shareholders and employees don't conflict, they align towards the creation of sustainable value. Organizations that understand this create win-win strategies where employee satisfaction and shareholder returns reinforce each other. Those that assume conflict create lose-lose outcomes where both suffer.

The Resolution: Employee Happiness AS Business Strategy

Reconciling profit with employee happiness doesn't require compromise or balance, it requires recognizing that employee happiness **IS** a profit-maximization strategy. Organizations that create genuine employee engagement don't sacrifice profitability for people; they achieve superior profitability **THROUGH** people.

The research evidence supporting this is overwhelming:

- Productivity Advantage: Happy workers demonstrate 12–13% higher productivity, as evidenced by large-scale field research conducted by the University of Oxford and published in Management Science (De Neve et al., 2023).
- Profitability Advantage: Organizations in the top quartile of employee engagement achieve approximately 21% higher profitability, according to extensive global meta-analysis conducted by Gallup (Gallup, 2020).
- Sales Advantage: Highly engaged organizations generate approximately 20% higher sales, reflecting stronger employee commitment, discretionary effort, and customer interactions (Gallup, 2020).
- Quality Advantage: Workforces with high engagement experience up to 40% fewer quality defects, highlighting the link between engagement, attention, and operational excellence (Gallup, 2020).
- Retention Advantage: Employee engagement is associated with 24–59% lower turnover, depending on industry and role type, reducing both direct and indirect replacement costs (Gallup, 2020).
- Innovation Advantage: Engaged organizations consistently report significantly higher innovation rates, as employees are more willing to contribute

ideas, take initiative, and collaborate creatively (De Neve et al., 2023; Cameron, 2012).

Customer Satisfaction Advantage: Organizations with highly engaged employees achieve approximately 10% higher customer ratings, reinforcing the service-profit chain linking employee experience to customer outcomes (Gallup, 2020). These aren't trivial differences, they're competitive advantages that compound over time into dominant market positions. Organizations achieving these advantages don't do so despite investing in employee happiness; they achieve them because of that investment.

The business case for employee happiness isn't that it's the right thing to do (though it is). It's that it's the smart thing to do, the strategy that produces superior financial results.

The New Framework: Stakeholder Capitalism

Recent years have seen growing recognition that the Friedman doctrine's exclusive focus on shareholders is both morally questionable and economically suboptimal. The stakeholder capitalism movement argues that companies should consider the interests of all stakeholders, employees, customers, suppliers, communities, environment, not just shareholders. This concept is popularized by the work of R. Edward Freeman (1984) and his Stakeholder Theory that provides the base for what many pro-employee companies and others are doing today.

This isn't altruism; it's enlightened self-interest. Companies that treat all stakeholders well create sustainable value that benefits shareholders over time. Companies that exploit stakeholders for short-term shareholder gain eventually face consequences, employee turnover, customer defection, supplier unreliability, community opposition, regulatory response.

The Business Roundtable's 2019 "Statement on the Purpose of a Corporation," signed by 181 CEO members, marked a significant shift. It explicitly moved away from shareholder primacy toward stakeholder consideration, stating that companies should deliver value to customers, invest in employees, deal fairly with suppliers, and support communities.

Whether this represents genuine philosophical shift or public relations positioning remains debatable. But the statement's existence acknowledges what research has long demonstrated: that sustainable business success requires attending to multiple stakeholders, including employees.

The Implementation Challenge

Understanding that employee happiness drives profitability is necessary but insufficient. Implementation requires overcoming several organizational obstacles:

Measurement: Organizations must measure employee happiness/engagement as rigorously as they measure financial metrics. What gets measured gets managed.

Accountability: Leaders must be held accountable for employee engagement through performance evaluations, compensation, and advancement decisions.

Resource Allocation: Budgets must reflect that employee engagement is an investment, not an expense, with resources protected even during difficult periods.

Time Horizon: Organizations must prioritize long-term value creation over short-term profit maximization, accepting that engagement investments may take time to show full returns.

Cultural Change: Organizations must shift from viewing employees as costs to minimize, toward viewing them as assets to develop, requiring fundamental cultural transformation.

Leadership Development: Organizations must develop leaders who have both the will and skill to create engagement, not just drive short-term results.

These challenges are real but surmountable. Organizations around the world demonstrate daily that it's possible to create highly engaged workforces while achieving excellent financial results. The question isn't whether it's possible but whether organizations will commit to the changes required.

The Competitive Imperative

Perhaps the most compelling argument for prioritizing employee happiness comes from competitive dynamics. Organizations that create genuine engagement while competitors don't achieve compounding advantages that eventually become insurmountable.

Initially, the advantages may seem modest, a few percentage points in productivity, slightly better retention, marginally higher innovation rates. But these advantages compound:

- Higher productivity enables better pricing or margins
- Better retention preserves knowledge and relationships
- Higher innovation creates new offerings and improves existing ones
- Superior customer service protects and grows market share
- Better employer brand attracts top talent while competitors struggle to hire

Over time, the gap widens. The engaged organization accelerates while competitors stagnate or decline. Eventually, the engaged organization dominates its market not through superior strategy or resources but through superior execution enabled by superior engagement.

In increasingly competitive markets where products are similar, technology is accessible, and operational excellence is table stakes, the differentiator becomes human capital. Organizations that unlock their people's full capability through engagement win. Those that leave the majority of human potential untapped lose.

The choice isn't whether to prioritize employee happiness, it's whether to achieve the competitive advantages that happiness enables or cede those advantages to competitors who understand this relationship.

Conclusion: The False Dichotomy Resolved

The apparent tension between profit maximization and employee happiness is false, created by outdated thinking, short-term focus, and flawed assumptions about human motivation and organizational performance.

Research thus far demonstrates unambiguously that:

- Employee happiness drives productivity, profitability, and performance
- Creating happiness doesn't require expensive perks but competent management
- Happy employees are more driven, not less
- Employee and shareholder interests align around value creation
- Companies excelling at engagement outperform competitors financially

Organizations that continue trading employee happiness for short term profit maximization are making a costly error. They're sacrificing the very thing that would improve profitability, engaged employees contributing their full capability.

The business case for employee happiness isn't sentimental or idealistic. It's hardheaded recognition that in knowledge economies where success depends on human creativity, problem-solving, and commitment, the organizations that best develop and engage their people achieve superior results.

The revolution isn't in recognizing that profit matters, everyone accepts that. The revolution is in recognizing that employee happiness IS how you achieve sustainable profit, not something you sacrifice to achieve it. Organizations that understand this truth don't need to reconcile profit with purpose, they recognize that in treating people well, they've found the path to both.

Chapter 5

The Responsibility Matrix: Who Owns Employee Happiness in the Modern Workplace?
(Whose Responsibility Is It to Influence Employee Happiness?)

So far, I have established that employee happiness drives organizational success and that organizations should prioritize it strategically. Now comes a practical question with profound implications: Who bears responsibility for creating employee happiness? Is it HR's job? Senior leadership's mandate? Employees' own responsibility? Or primarily the role of direct managers?

The research points clearly to an answer, though the implications make many leaders uncomfortable: managers, specifically direct supervisors, bear primary responsibility for employee happiness and engagement. This chapter explores why this is true, what the evidence shows, and what it means for organizational design and management practice.

Understanding responsibility distribution matters because misplaced responsibility leads to failed interventions. Organizations that assign happiness responsibility to HR create programs that managers ignore. Organizations that expect employees to manage their own happiness blame victims for systemic failures. Organizations that rely on senior leaders to create happiness through vision and values discover that inspiring speeches don't compensate for poor daily management.

Getting responsibility right, placing it primarily where research shows it belongs, is prerequisite for effective action.

The Survey Data: Management's Motivation Failure

My research survey documents systematic management failure to fulfill basic motivational responsibilities:

15.54% Say Management Never Motivates Them

More than 20 million American workers report that their managers provide zero motivational support. Not occasionally. Not inconsistently. Never. These employees show up, perform tasks, and go home without their managers ever attempting to engage, inspire, or energize them.

This represents fundamental dereliction of management responsibility. Motivation isn't a nice-to-have aspect of management, it's a core function. Managers who never motivate aren't managing; they're administering tasks while abdicating leadership.

I have witnessed specific instances where "managers" have held an in-person meeting once with their team in a span of two years. Two years! I have witnessed "managers" threaten to place a letter in the personal file of an employee because the employee was taking initiative on a new project. The manager threatened such because the employee didn't follow some fantasy procedure that supposedly existed, though no one else knew of the procedure in question. I have witnessed "managers" never saying a word to their employees even though they pass them every day in the office.

Q2: How often does management personally motivate you in your current job role?

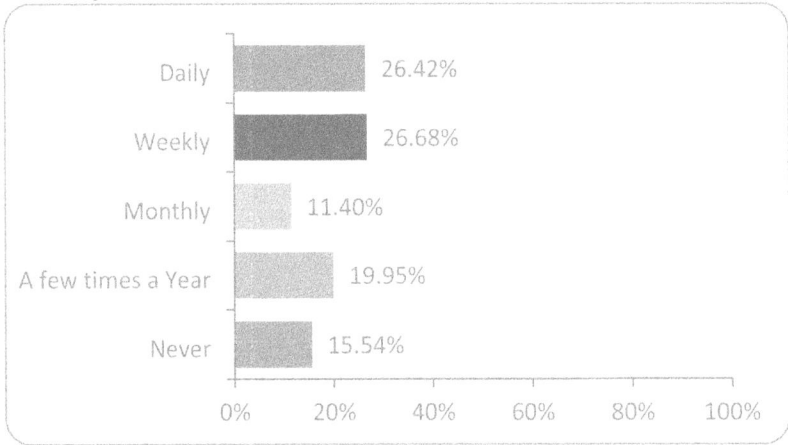

Daily	26.42%
Weekly	26.68%
Monthly	11.40%
A few times a Year	19.95%
Never	15.54%

0%   20%   40%   60%   80%   100%

31.87% Rank Management as Their Last Source of Motivation

When asked to rank five given attributes that motivates them at work, 31.87% of respondents ranked management last among all options. This was the highest recorded answer in all combinations. Think about what this means: nearly 43 million workers find their managers to be the least motivating factor in their work lives, less motivating than the work itself, colleagues, compensation, or recognition programs.

This data point is particularly damning because it reveals not just absence of motivation but active demotivation. These aren't employees saying management is neutral; they're saying management is the factor they turn to last when seeking motivation. The implicit message: managers actively undermine rather than support motivation.

Q3: In order of effectiveness, 1 being most effective, what factors motivate you the best at work?

	1	2	3	4	5	TOTAL	SCORE
Management	15.54%	12.18%	18.39%	22.02%	31.87%		
	60	47	71	85	123	386	2.58
Recognition and rewards	27.72%	18.39%	17.36%	16.84%	19.69%		
	107	71	67	65	76	386	3.18
Work environment	23.58%	26.42%	25.39%	14.77%	9.84%		
	91	102	98	57	38	386	3.39
Colleagues and teamwork	17.10%	22.28%	22.02%	25.39%	13.21%		
	66	86	85	98	51	386	3.05
Personal growth and development	16.06%	20.73%	16.84%	20.98%	25.39%		
	62	80	65	81	98	386	2.81

38.08% Rate Management's Purposeful Motivation Efforts as Poor or Absent

When asked to rate how purposefully management acts to motivate them, 38.08% responded "poor," "very poor," or "not purposeful at all." Within this group, 16.32% said management makes no purposeful effort to motivate them whatsoever, approximately 22 million workers whose managers don't even attempt to engage them.

This reveals that management motivation failures aren't accidental. They're not managers trying hard but failing. They're managers not trying at all, treating employee motivation as outside their responsibility or beneath their concern.

I celebrate the nearly 62% that give management a positive rating. This is great news! The opportunity in front of us is with the 38.08%, or more than 51,000,000 workers who are not getting positive nudges, inspiring suggestions or encouragement from their managers.

Q7: How would you rate purposeful actions by management to motivate you?

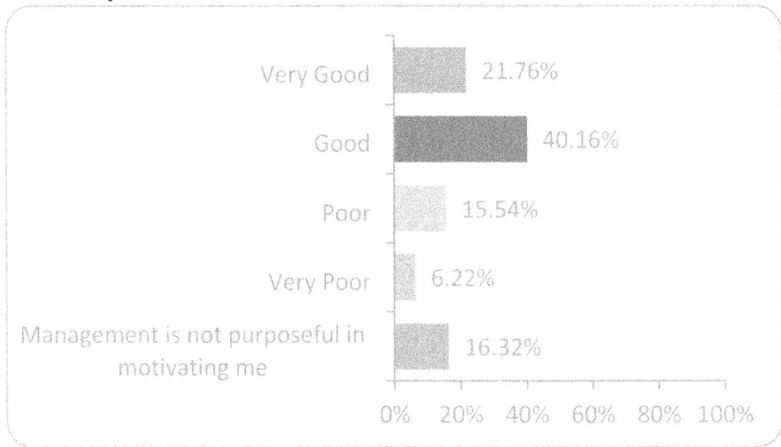

Very Good	21.76%
Good	40.16%
Poor	15.54%
Very Poor	6.22%
Management is not purposeful in motivating me	16.32%

Julie Zhuo (The Making of a Manager) writes "The best outcomes come from inspiring people to action, not telling them what to do." Granted, we are ultimately in charge of ourselves. Clay Scroggins (How to Lead When You're Not in Charge) quotes Thomas Watson "Nothing so conclusively proves a man's ability to lead others as what he does on a day-to-day basis to lead himself". However, managers and leaders are in a position to motivate others. John C. Maxwell (5 Levels of Leadership) writes "As an experienced leader, you can identify potential leaders, you can figure out what kinds of experiences they need, and you can help to provide them in a controlled environment where their failures and fumbles won't completely take them out of the game of leadership".

27.46% Don't Trust Their Managers

More than one in four employees, approximately 37 million American workers, do not trust their direct managers. Trust is foundational to all leadership effectiveness. Without trust, communication fails, feedback is rejected, direction is resisted, and influence is impossible.

Q9: Do you trust your manager?

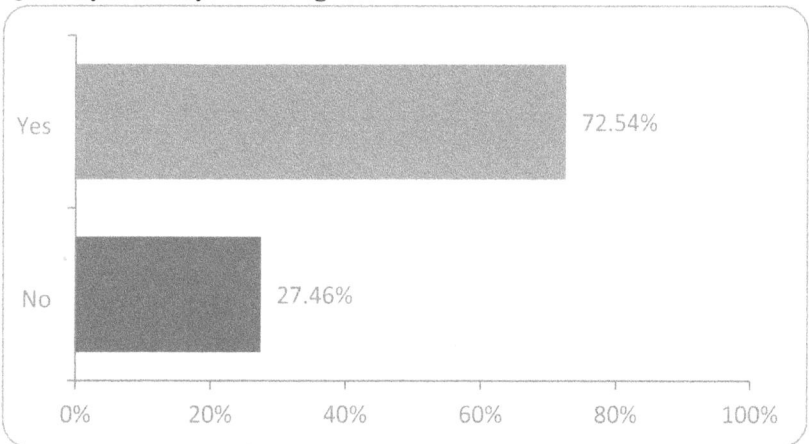

When almost a quarter of the workforce doesn't trust their immediate supervisors, we're documenting systemic leadership failure. These trust failures don't emerge randomly, they result from managers who lie, break promises, play favorites, take credit for others' work, or protect themselves at their team's expense.

The Theoretical Foundation: Why Managers Matter Most

Research across organizational psychology, management science, and leadership studies consistently identifies direct managers as the primary determinant of employee engagement. Multiple factors explain why:

Proximity and Frequency

Direct managers interact with employees far more frequently than senior leaders or HR. These daily interactions, how managers communicate, respond to questions, handle mistakes, recognize contributions, and treat people, shape employee experience more than infrequent interactions with senior leadership or HR.

The cumulative effect of hundreds of small interactions dwarfs the impact of occasional all-hands meetings or annual HR initiatives. An inspiring CEO speech might motivate temporarily, but a manager's dismissive comment the next day neutralizes any positive effect.

Control Over Work Experience

Direct managers control most aspects of employees' daily work experience:
- What work gets assigned and how it's framed
- What support and resources are provided
- How performance is evaluated and feedback delivered

- Whether contributions are recognized or ignored
- How mistakes are handled
- What development opportunities are offered
- How autonomy is granted or restricted
- Whether voice is welcomed or suppressed

These factors directly affect whether employees find work meaningful, feel competent, experience autonomy, and feel valued, the core elements of workplace happiness.

Relationship Quality

The quality of the manager-employee relationship predicts engagement more strongly than almost any other variable. Employees with managers who they trust, respect, and feel cared for by show dramatically higher engagement than those with managers they distrust, disrespect, or feel uncared for by.

Research on leader–member exchange (LMX) theory demonstrates that the quality of relationships between managers and employees significantly influences performance, satisfaction, commitment, and retention, with high-quality exchanges characterized by trust and mutual respect predicting positive outcomes and low-quality exchanges predicting poorer outcomes (Graen & Uhl-Bien, 1995; Mary Uhl-Bien, 2012).

Psychological Safety Creation

Psychological safety, the sense that it's safe to take interpersonal risks like asking questions, admitting mistakes, or challenging ideas, depends primarily on direct manager behavior. Research by Amy Edmondson (1999) demonstrates that leaders create psychological safety through their responses to voice, mistakes, and challenges.

Managers who welcome questions, thank people for identifying problems, and respond constructively to mistakes create safety. Managers who react defensively to questions, punish problem identification, and blame people for mistakes destroy safety. HR programs can't create safety that daily management interactions destroy.

Modeling and Culture Transmission

Direct managers translate organizational culture and values into daily reality through their behavior. Employees learn what the organization values by watching what managers reward, punish, and ignore. Mission statements and value lists matter less than what managers consistently reinforce through their actions.

When organizational values say "we value innovation" but managers punish failed experiments, employees learn innovation isn't valued. When values emphasize "people first" but managers prioritize output regardless of human cost, employees learn people aren't actually first. Managers' behavior, not corporate rhetoric, defines culture.

Supporting Research: Shawn Achor's Argument

Shawn Achor's (2010) research on positive psychology and organizational success explicitly argues that managers hold primary responsibility for employee happiness. His work demonstrates that creating positive emotions and engagement isn't an individual employee responsibility, it requires supportive environmental conditions that managers control.

Achor identifies specific managerial practices that create engagement:
- Recognizing contributions authentically and specifically
- Helping employees see meaning in their work
- Creating positive social connections within teams
- Focusing on strengths rather than fixing weaknesses
- Reframing challenges as opportunities
- Modeling optimism and resilience

These aren't individual employee practices, they're management responsibilities requiring conscious effort and skill. Employees can't create these conditions independently; they require managers who understand their importance and commit to implementing them.

The Gallup Perspective: Five Drivers of Engagement

Gallup's (2022) extensive engagement research identifies five primary drivers of employee engagement: purpose, development opportunities, a caring manager, ongoing conversations, and a focus on strengths. Notably, managers directly influence or control four of the five:

Purpose: While organizational mission provides context, managers help employees connect their specific work to meaningful outcomes. The same task can feel meaningful or meaningless depending on how managers frame it and whether they help employees see impact.

Development: Managers largely control what developmental opportunities employees receive, stretch assignments, skill-building projects, coaching, mentoring, and training. Organizations may provide resources, but managers determine who gets access.

Caring Manager: This driver explicitly names managers. Employees need to feel their managers genuinely care about them as humans, not just as producers. This can't be programmed or systematized, it requires individual managers who actually care and demonstrate it consistently. Imagine if an employee had a death in their family and their immediate manager never mentioned a word of condolence to the employee in person.

Ongoing Conversations: Regular, high-quality conversations between managers and employees about performance, development, and career create engagement. Annual reviews don't substitute for ongoing dialogue that managers must initiate and maintain. If your manager is only meeting with your once a year to review your performance, they are being lazy and uncaring of your growth and contributions.

Focus on Strengths: Managers determine whether they focus on building employees' strengths or fixing weaknesses. Research shows strengths-based management creates much higher engagement, but it requires managers who identify and develop strengths rather than defaulting to weakness-fixing.

HR's Supporting Role

While managers hold primary responsibility, HR plays a crucial enabling role. HR influences engagement through:

System Design: HR creates policies, processes, and programs that either support or undermine manager effectiveness. Well-designed systems make good management easier; poorly designed systems make it harder.

Manager Development: HR provides training, coaching, and development that builds managers' capability to create engagement. Many managers have never been taught how to motivate, develop, or engage people, HR can fill this gap.

Measurement and Accountability: HR designs engagement measurement systems and incorporates engagement metrics into manager performance evaluations, creating accountability.

Resource Provision: HR provides tools, programs, and resources that support engagement, recognition platforms, development programs, communication systems.

Problem Identification: HR aggregates engagement data to identify problematic patterns, departments or managers with persistent low engagement who need intervention.

However, HR can't create engagement that daily management destroys. HR programs and policies matter, but manager behavior matters more. The best-designed recognition program fails if managers don't use it. The most generous development budget fails if managers don't provide opportunities. The most inspiring mission and values fail if managers contradict them daily.

Employee Agency and Responsibility

While managers play a primary role in shaping the conditions for employee happiness, research indicates that employees retain significant agency, with dispositional and intentional factors accounting for a substantial proportion, often estimated at around 40–50%, of job satisfaction and daily well-being (Timothy A. Judge et al., 2001; Sonja Lyubomirsky et al., 2005).

Employees can influence their own happiness through:

Relationship Building: Proactively building friendships at work creates social support that buffers against stress and increases satisfaction. Research by Gallup (2022) shows having a best friend at work significantly predicts engagement.

Meaning Making: Employees can frame their work in ways that highlight meaning and purpose. Research shows that consciously connecting daily tasks to valued outcomes increases satisfaction.

Strengths Application: Employees who find ways to apply their strengths more frequently experience higher engagement, even when formal job design doesn't emphasize those strengths.

Learning Orientation: Approaching work with a growth mindset, seeing challenges as opportunities to develop rather than threats, affects satisfaction regardless of circumstances.

Boundary Setting: Employees who establish and maintain healthy boundaries between work and personal life experience better wellbeing and sustained engagement.

However, employee agency operates within constraints that managers largely determine. Employees can't create meaning in work that managers frame as meaningless. They can't build relationships in toxic cultures that managers create. They can't apply strengths in roles that managers rigidly define. They can't maintain boundaries when managers expect 24/7 availability.

Employee responsibility complements but doesn't replace manager responsibility. Expecting employees to create their own happiness despite poor management is blaming victims for systemic failures.

Senior Leadership's Role

Senior leaders play an important but indirect role in employee happiness. They create conditions that enable or prevent manager effectiveness:

Culture Setting: Senior leaders establish organizational culture through their values, priorities, and behavior. Culture cascades down, affecting how all managers behave.

System Design: Senior leaders approve policies, structures, and processes that either support or undermine engagement.

Decisions about span of control, decision authority, resource allocation, and performance management systems affect manager effectiveness.

Role Modeling: Senior leaders model priorities through how they spend time, what they reward, and what they tolerate. If senior leaders work 70-hour weeks, ignore work-life balance, and prioritize results regardless of human cost, managers throughout the organization will mirror these behaviors.

Resource Allocation: Senior leaders control budgets that determine what resources are available for development, recognition, communication, and other engagement-supporting activities.

Accountability Creation: Senior leaders determine whether engagement becomes a real accountability for managers through performance evaluation, promotion decisions, and consequences for persistent low engagement.

However, senior leadership influence is mediated through managers. Inspiring vision from the CEO doesn't compensate for a toxic immediate supervisor. Generous budgets from executives don't help if managers don't use resources well. Clear values from leadership fail if managers contradict them daily.

The Research Consensus: 95% Hold Managers Responsible

Research conducted by EtherWorld (2024) found that 95% of employees feel managers hold primary responsibility for ensuring their happiness at work. This represents remarkable consensus, employees across industries, roles, and demographics agree that their direct supervisors bear primary responsibility for their workplace experience.

This consensus matters because it reflects lived experience. Employees interact with managers daily and experience firsthand how manager behavior affects their engagement, motivation, and satisfaction. They know that HR programs matter less than manager implementation, that senior leader vision matters less than immediate supervisor support, and that their own agency operates within constraints largely determined by management.

When 95% of workers agree on something, dismissing their perspective is foolish. The consensus reflects reality that research confirms: managers matter most.

The Uncomfortable Implications

Accepting that managers hold primary responsibility for employee happiness creates several uncomfortable implications for organizations:

Selection Implications: Organizations must select managers based partly on their capacity and willingness to create engagement, not solely on technical competence or individual achievement. The best individual contributor often makes a terrible manager.

Development Implications: Organizations must invest substantially in developing managers' people leadership capabilities. Technical training isn't sufficient, managers need development in motivation, communication, coaching, feedback, and relationship building.

Evaluation Implications: Organizations must evaluate managers partly on team engagement and development, not solely on team output. Managers who hit numbers while destroying morale should be held accountable, not celebrated.

Compensation Implications: Organizations should tie meaningful portions of manager compensation to team engagement metrics. If engagement matters, managers should feel financial consequences for ignoring it.

Accountability Implications: Organizations must address managers who persistently fail to create engagement. Tolerating toxic managers because they deliver results sends a clear message: results matter more than people.

Structural Implications: Organizations must ensure manager spans of control allow time for the relationship building, coaching, and development that engagement requires. Managers overseeing 15-20+ people can't possibly provide the support engagement requires.

These implications challenge common practices. Many organizations promote based primarily on individual achievement, provide minimal management development, evaluate primarily on output metrics, and tolerate toxic high-performers. Accepting manager responsibility for happiness requires changing these practices.

The Psychosocial Safety Climate Framework

Recent research on Psychosocial Safety Climate (PSC) provides additional theoretical support for manager responsibility. PSC theory, developed by Dollard and Bakker (2010), describes PSC as an "upstream factor" determining job demands, resources, worker engagement, and psychological health.

PSC operates largely through management and leadership. Employees perceive four aspects of PSC:

- Support from senior management for psychological health
- Prioritization of employee psychological health over productivity
- Communication about psychological health and safety
- Participation in psychological health and safety discussions

All four aspects involve management behavior. Senior management demonstrates support through actions, not statements. Prioritization is revealed through daily decisions that managers make. Communication happens through manager-employee interactions. Participation is facilitated by managers who welcome voice and involvement.

Research shows PSC predicts job demands, resources, engagement, and health outcomes (Dollard & Bakker, 2010; Law et al., 2011). Organizations with high PSC, where managers genuinely prioritize psychological health, achieve better outcomes across all measures. Organizations with low PSC, where managers prioritize output regardless of psychological cost, suffer predictable consequences (Zadow et al., 2017).

The framework reinforces that employee happiness isn't accidental or individual, it results from organizational and management practices that either support or undermine psychological health.

Conclusion: Clarity on Responsibility

The research evidence is clear and consistent: direct managers hold primary responsibility for employee happiness and engagement. They don't bear sole responsibility, HR, senior leadership, and employees themselves all play roles. But managers' role is primary because they:

- Interact with employees most frequently
- Control most aspects of daily work experience
- Create or destroy psychological safety through their responses (Edmondson, 1999)
- Translate organizational culture into daily reality
- Build or undermine trust through their behavior

Organizations that accept this reality and act accordingly, selecting managers for people leadership capacity, developing their engagement creation skills, evaluating them on team engagement, and holding them accountable for persistent failures, create conditions for happiness. Those that continue treating management as primarily technical role while expecting HR or employees to create happiness achieve predictably poor results.

The 95% employee consensus isn't wrong. The extensive research confirming manager primacy isn't mistaken. The question isn't whether managers hold primary responsibility, the evidence says they clearly do. The question is whether organizations will act on this knowledge by ensuring managers have the capability, support, and accountability to fulfill this responsibility effectively.

Getting responsibility right is prerequisite for improvement. Organizations that continue misplacing responsibility, expecting HR programs or employee resilience to overcome poor management, waste resources on interventions that can't succeed. Organizations that accept manager responsibility and invest accordingly can achieve the engagement advantages that drive superior performance.

The choice, as always, is whether to act on what research clearly demonstrates or continue hoping that alternative approaches somehow produce different results.

Chapter 6

The Manager's Toolkit: Evidence-Based Strategies for Fostering Employee Happiness
(If Managers Should Influence Employee Happiness, How Can They Do This?)

The previous chapter established that managers bear primary responsibility for employee happiness. Now comes the practical question: What exactly should managers do? How do they translate responsibility into action? What specific practices create engagement?

This chapter provides an evidence-based toolkit, strategies grounded in research that managers can implement regardless of personality type, industry, or organizational context. Creating employee happiness doesn't require charisma, extroversion, or exceptional emotional intelligence. It requires understanding and consistently applying practices that research has proven effective.

The good news for introverted, analytical, or technically-oriented managers: these aren't mysterious soft skills that some people have and others don't. They're learnable, practicable behaviors that any manager can master with commitment and practice.

Social Psychological Influences: Understanding Emotional Contagion

Research on emotional contagion demonstrates that emotions spread between people through unconscious processes, with leaders' emotional states significantly influencing team emotional climate (Barsade & Gibson, 2012).

The Neuroscience of Mirroring

Research suggests mirror neurons in human brains activate both when performing actions and observing others perform them (Rizzolatti & Craighero, 2004). This neural mirroring may extend beyond actions to emotional states (Bastiaansen et al., 2009). When team members observe stressed, anxious managers, evidence indicates their brains may simulate that stress (Hatfield et al., 1994).

When observing calm confidence, similar neural simulation likely occurs. Research documents this through physiological measures (Sy et al., 2005). Teams whose managers display chronic stress often show elevated cortisol levels even without directly experiencing stressors (Hoobler & Brass, 2006). Teams whose managers model calm problem-solving tend to show lower baseline stress markers. The practical implication: managers likely conduct emotional orchestras whether they realize it or not. Walking into meetings stressed and frantic may elevate team stress. Demonstrating composed problem-solving appears to create team calmness. The emotional tone managers set often cascades throughout their teams.

Social Proof and Behavioral Modeling

People take behavioral cues from authority figures through social proof, the tendency to follow others' behaviors, especially those with status or authority. Managers model what's acceptable, expected, and valued through their behavior more than their words.

If managers never take breaks, teams won't take breaks. If managers check e-mail at midnight, teams feel expected to do the same. If managers treat mistakes as catastrophes, teams hide errors. Every behavior managers display becomes implicit permission or prohibition.

Edmondson's (1999) research on psychological safety demonstrates this clearly. Teams feel safe taking risks when managers model vulnerability by admitting their own mistakes, asking for help, and acknowledging uncertainty. Teams fear risks when managers project infallibility and punish errors.

The practical application: managers should consciously model behaviors they want to see. Want teams to maintain work-life balance? Model it by setting boundaries. Want teams to admit mistakes early? Model it by openly acknowledging your own. Want teams to ask questions? Model it by asking questions publicly.

Recognition and Rewards: Addressing the Core Motivator

Survey data revealed that 27.72% of employees, more than one in four, identify recognition and rewards as their primary motivator. Yet 48.19% say recognition programs are ineffective or nonexistent. This gap represents massive untapped potential.

Q3: In order of effectiveness, 1 being most effective, what factors motivate you best at work?

	1	2	3	4	5	TOTAL	SCORE
Management	15.54% 60	12.18% 47	18.39% 71	22.02% 85	31.87% 123	386	2.58
Recognition and rewards	27.72% 107	18.39% 71	17.36% 67	16.84% 65	19.69% 76	386	3.18
Work environment	23.58% 91	26.42% 102	25.39% 98	14.77% 57	9.84% 38	386	3.39
Colleagues and teamwork	17.10% 66	22.28% 86	22.02% 85	25.39% 98	13.21% 51	386	3.05
Personal growth and development	16.06% 62	20.73% 80	16.84% 65	20.98% 81	25.39% 98	386	2.81

The Research on Effective Recognition

Decades of psychological research on motivation and reinforcement identify specific characteristics that make recognition effective versus ineffective:

Specificity: Generic praise like "good job" registers barely above neutral. Specific recognition naming exactly what was valuable and why creates lasting impact. "Your analysis identified a trend that changed our product roadmap" is dramatically more effective than "nice work."

Q6: How effective are the recognition and reward programs in your organization?

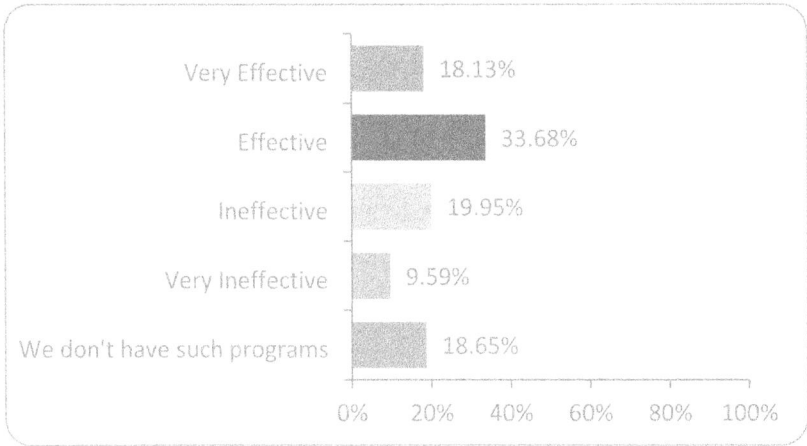

Very Effective	18.13%
Effective	33.68%
Ineffective	19.95%
Very Ineffective	9.59%
We don't have such programs	18.65%

Timeliness: Recognition delivered immediately after achievements creates dopamine responses that reinforce behaviors. Delayed recognition requires conscious memory retrieval and provides minimal motivational boost. The half-life of recognition impact drops dramatically after 48 hours.

Authenticity: Employees detect insincere recognition instantly, and insincere recognition is worse than none. It signals that you view recognition as manipulation rather than genuine appreciation, destroying trust.

Personalization: Some people value public recognition; others find it mortifying and prefer private acknowledgment. Some want written recognition they can save; others prefer verbal appreciation. One-size-fits-all recognition fits nobody well.

Frequency: Reinforcement principles suggest that frequent, specific recognition may be more effective than infrequent large awards, though more research is needed to establish optimal recognition frequency in workplace settings.

The Implementation Gap

Understanding what makes recognition effective doesn't guarantee implementation. The gap between knowing and doing explains why recognition programs fail. Organizations create formal systems, employee-of-the-month, annual awards, digital kudos platforms, while neglecting informal, authentic, immediate manager recognition.

The take-away is clear: manager-delivered, specific, timely, authentic recognition matters more than formal programs. Programs can support but not substitute for managers who pay attention and express genuine appreciation consistently. Effective recognition requires both manager commitment and organizational support. While formal recognition programs provide structure and resources, the interpersonal relationship between manager and employee remains central to engagement outcomes (Harter, et al., 2002).

Communication Excellence: The Foundation of Management

Only 22.02% of employees rate management communication as "very good," while 30.83% rate it as poor or very poor. This represents systematic failure at a core management function.

Patrick Lencioni shared a post on LinkedIn on November 16th, 2025 that read "The hidden danger of leadership isn't failure. It's comfort. When leaders avoid hard conversations or difficult decisions, they're not protecting peace. They're protecting themselves." This resonates deeply with the results of my research as nearly half of the respondents gave communication from management poor scores.

Q10: How would you rate open and authentic communication from management to employees?

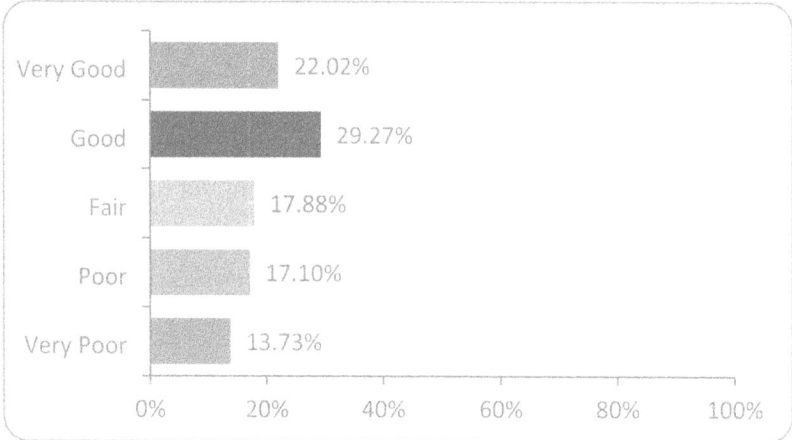

Very Good	22.02%
Good	29.27%
Fair	17.88%
Poor	17.10%
Very Poor	13.73%

In an age of unprecedented technological advancement, it's astonishing that communication between leadership and their teams remains so deeply flawed. And with the rapid integration of artificial intelligence, the stakes are only getting higher. In AI First, Adam Brotman and Andy Sack caution that AI won't usher in incremental progress, but rather "a sudden and fundamental shift in how businesses are able to increase both the speed and the quality of their decision-making" (p.42-43).

If communication is already broken, what happens when decisions accelerate and employees are left even further behind?

Charles Duhigg, in his 2024 book Supercommunicators, offers a hopeful roadmap. In Chapter 7, he explores how to approach hard conversations, emphasizing that discomfort is temporary but essential. Duhigg brings up identity threat and how it can be corrosive to communication. When leaders stay silent, are they grouping employees into a population that doesn't matter? I think the case could be made that this is so.

And that's the danger. My survey didn't ask about "hard" conversations, just general communication, yet nearly half of employees still gave poor ratings.

So here's the question:

Does your leadership team communicate with you regularly and authentically?

If the answer is yes, celebrate it. It's a gift. More than 65 million workers across this country can't say the same.

What Effective Communication Requires

Foundations of organizational communication identify several characteristics distinguishing effective from ineffective management communication:

Purposefulness: Every communication should serve clear purpose, to inform, clarify, seek input, build alignment, or address concerns. Communication for its own sake creates noise that drowns receptive meaning. Survey respondents specifically noted that "communication should be purposeful."

Clarity Over Volume: More communication isn't better if it's unclear, contradictory, or confusing. Employees prefer less information that's clear over more that's ambiguous. Research (Men, 2014; Johlke & Duhan, 2000) shows communication quality predicts engagement more strongly than communication frequency.

Bidirectional Flow: Communication flowing only downward, from management to employees, misses critical information flowing upward and fails to create understanding. Research shows that questions, feedback, and dialogue transform information delivery into mutual understanding.

Consistency: Regular, predictable communication creates trust while sporadic, unpredictable communication generates anxiety. When employees know when they'll get information, they worry less. When communication is random, they worry constantly.

Transparency: Employees understand managers can't share everything, confidential information, pending decisions, competitive sensitive data. What employees can't tolerate is feeling managers could share but choose not to, or worse, actively hide information.

The Silence Crisis

I have always felt that silence is a form of abuse in the workplace as it "alienates and causes worry." This isn't hyperbole. Research on uncertainty and anxiety (Bordia, Hunt, Paulsen, Tourish, & DiFonzo, 2004) demonstrates that information voids get filled with imagination, and imagination tends toward worst-case scenarios.

When managers stay silent, employees create narratives to explain the silence: hiding bad news, lacking care, being too busy, or not valuing employees enough to communicate. All interpretations are negative. Even when silence stems from benign causes, legitimate busy-ness, waiting for complete information, employees interpret it as problematic.

The solution is proactive communication, even when information is incomplete. "I don't have full information yet, but here's what I know, when I expect to know more, and what I'm doing to get answers" eliminates anxiety better than silence while awaiting perfect information.

Tailored Communication

Research on learning styles and communication preferences shows people process information differently. Some are highly analytical and prefer detailed written communication they can study. Some are more emotional and need verbal conversation to understand nuance. Some are visual and want diagrams and examples.

Delivering the same message identically to everyone guarantees it lands well with some and poorly with others.

Effective communicators adapt their approach based on how different people best receive and process information.

This requires actually knowing team members well enough to understand their preferences, another reason why relationship quality predicts management effectiveness.

The Power of Reframing: Changing Workplace Perspectives

Emerson wrote: "To different minds, the same world is a hell, and a heaven." This captures a profound truth: perception matters as much as reality. Research on cognitive reframing demonstrates that how people interpret their work dramatically affects their experience of it.

Meaning Making

Research consistently shows that meaningful work generates higher engagement, satisfaction, and intrinsic motivation (Rosso, Dekas, & Wrzesniewski, 2010; Steger, Dik, & Duffy, 2012). Two people doing identical tasks can have wildly different experiences based entirely on how they frame the work's meaning and purpose.

The classic example involves three stonemasons. Asked what they're doing, one says "cutting stones," another says "building a wall," and the third says "building a cathedral that will inspire generations." Same work, dramatically different frames, profoundly different experiences.

Managers influence meaning by connecting daily tasks to valued outcomes. "This code you're writing helps small business owners process payments faster, letting them spend time with families instead of fighting software" transforms "writing code" into "enabling dreams." Same work, different frame, transformed experience.

Challenge Versus Burden

Research on growth mindset demonstrates that how people frame challenges affects their response (Dweck, 2006; Caniëls, Semeijn, & Renders, 2018). Challenges viewed as opportunities for growth generate engagement and persistence. Challenges viewed as burdens generate anxiety and avoidance.

Managers influence framing through language and response. "This project will stretch your capabilities and develop new skills" frames identically to "This project is difficult and will require working harder" yet creates completely different psychological experiences. Near my hometown, Tom Sawyer made painting a fence seem like so much fun, he got others to do it for him.

Honesty and Organizational Transparency: Building Trust

Research on organizational justice demonstrates that perceptions of fairness, in how decisions are made, how resources are distributed, and how information is shared, profoundly affect engagement and satisfaction.

The Trust Foundation

Trust forms the foundation of all leadership effectiveness. Without trust, communication is discounted, feedback is rejected, direction is resisted, and influence is impossible. My survey found 27.46% of employees don't trust their managers which documents massive leadership failure.

Q9: Do you trust your manager?

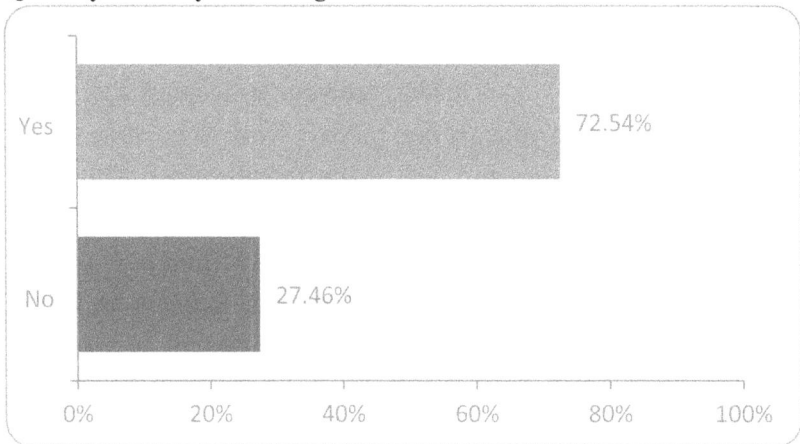

Trust builds through consistency between words and actions, honesty even when truth is uncomfortable, keeping commitments regardless of convenience, and admitting mistakes rather than hiding them.

I often quote and show clips of Brian Buffini in my sales class. In one of his past blog posts, Mr. Buffini writes "To become a trusted advisor to your clients, you must consistently show them that you respect and value them, you're personally invested and you'll always go the extra mile, not just during the transaction, but beforehand and afterwards too. Every small interaction you have will either increase or decrease the trust between you." The same is true for leaders seeking to establish trust with their employees.

Julie Zhou (The Making of a Manager) writes "Only when you have built trust with your reports will you have the credibility to help them achieve more together." (p.36) She continues "A hallmark of a trusting relationship is that people feel they can share their mistakes, challenges and fear with you." (p.61) As a leader, are your colleagues sharing these things with you? If not, there is work to be done. Lou Holtz (Wins, Losses and Lessons) offers three questions of Can I trust you? Are you committed to excellence? Do you care about me? as indicators, if answered affirmative, that a person is a good leader among other roles. Stephen M. R. Covey (Trust & Inspire) writes "(As opposed to command and control)...a Trust and Inspire culture is the ultimate magnet for attracting top talent, because people are drawn to environments and cultures where they're trusted and free....High performers want to be where they'll be trusted and are empowered." (p.45).

Appropriate Transparency

Transparency doesn't mean sharing everything with everyone. Some information must remain confidential for legal, competitive, or ethical reasons. What transparency means is being honest about what you can share, what you can't, and why.

Research on organizational transparency shows that honest communication about information limitations builds trust more effectively than withholding information without explanation (Schnackenberg & Tomlinson, 2016). What destroys trust is suspecting that managers could share but choose not to, or worse, that managers are actively spinning or hiding information (Men & Stacks, 2014). I once asked for some numbers at work and my manager refused to give them to me because I didn't ask in the "right way". Even upon my apology for such "error" I was still refused the numbers even though they were directly related to my scope of responsibility.

The framework for appropriate transparency includes:

- What I know: Share confirmed information immediately
- What I don't know: Admit uncertainty rather than speculate
- What I can't share: Explain why without being mysterious
- When I'll know more: Set expectations for updates

This approach maintains trust even when full transparency isn't possible (Rawlins, 2008)

Ethical and Transformational Leadership: Inspiring Through Vision and Development

Research on transformational leadership demonstrates that leaders who inspire through vision, invest in development, and act with integrity create more engaged and productive teams.

Beyond Transactional Management

Transactional leadership, do this, get that, creates compliance but not engagement. People contribute exactly what's required for specified rewards but nothing beyond.

Transformational leadership inspires people to contribute beyond transactional requirements by connecting work to meaningful vision, investing in their development, and treating them as whole humans rather than as role performers. One of my best leaders always sold us on what was needed rather than telling us or directing us.

Research consistently shows transformational leadership predicts higher engagement, satisfaction, performance, and retention compared to purely transactional approaches (Breevaart et al., 2014; Wang, Oh, Courtright, & Colbert, 2011).

Individual Development Plans

Generic training programs provide baseline capabilities, but genuine development requires individualized approaches recognizing that different people need different development.

Effective managers can create individual development plans that:

- Identify each person's specific growth goals and aspirations

- Connect current work to development objectives
- Provide stretch opportunities that challenge without overwhelming
- Offer coaching, mentoring, and feedback tailored to individual needs
- Allocate time and resources for learning and development

This personalization requires knowing team members as individuals, understanding their aspirations, and investing time in their growth.

Motivation and Goal Setting: Creating Clear Pathways

Research on goal-setting theory, developed by Locke and Latham (2002), provides robust evidence that specific, challenging, achievable goals improve performance significantly compared to vague goals or no goals.

The SMART Framework and Beyond

Effective goals are Specific, Measurable, Achievable, Relevant, and Time-bound. This framework has become nearly universal because research validates it consistently. I continue to preach the SMART acronym in my marketing and sales courses to my students.

Locke & Latham (2002) offer effective goal-setting extends beyond SMART criteria to include:

Participative Goal Setting: People commit far more strongly to goals they help set than to goals imposed on them. Locke & Latham (2002) offer collaborative goal-setting creates ownership.

Regular Progress Feedback: Goals without feedback about progress leave people guessing whether they're succeeding. Regular check-ins enable course correction and maintain motivation.

Connection to Meaning: Goals explicitly connected to meaningful outcomes engage intrinsic motivation. Goals that feel arbitrary or disconnected reduce motivation.

Learning Goals for Complex Tasks: For simple tasks, performance goals work well. For complex tasks requiring creativity or problem-solving, learning goals, "identify three new approaches to this problem", may be more effective than performance goals.

Positive Thinking and Behavioral Modeling: Creating Optimistic Environments

Research on emotional contagion and social modeling demonstrates that leaders' emotional states and behaviors spread throughout teams (Barsade & Gibson, 2012). Managers who consistently model positive emotions, optimism, and resilience create team cultures characterized by similar states. Studies show that leaders' positive affective displays influence team members' emotions and subsequently impact team performance and collaboration (Chi, Chung, & Tsai, 2011). The effect is particularly strong for leaders, as their formal authority and visibility make their emotional expressions especially salient to team members.

Optimism Versus Toxic Positivity

Important distinction: optimism isn't denying problems or pretending difficulties don't exist. It's approaching problems with agency, believing that effort, strategy, and persistence can influence outcomes, rather than helplessness.

Research on explanatory styles shows that people who attribute setbacks to specific, temporary, and external causes maintain motivation and resilience better than those who attribute setbacks to global, permanent, and internal causes (Seligman, 1990). This optimistic explanatory style protects against helplessness and promotes adaptive coping when facing challenges. Managers model optimistic explanations by treating setbacks as specific ("this approach didn't work") rather than global ("nothing works"), temporary ("this time it failed") rather than permanent ("it always fails"), and solvable ("what can we try differently") rather than hopeless ("there's nothing we can do"). This modeling shapes how team members interpret and respond to their own setbacks.

Celebration of Progress

Research shows that making progress in meaningful work, even small incremental progress, is a primary driver of positive emotions and sustained motivation (Amabile & Kramer, 2011). Teams that acknowledge progress alongside addressing shortfalls maintain engagement through long projects more effectively than teams that only recognize achievement when everything is perfect.

Managers create this through deliberate practice of recognizing incremental progress, not just final outcomes.

Feedback and One-on-One Engagement: Building Individual Connections

Regular one-on-ones between managers and employees provide powerful opportunities to influence happiness through personalized attention, individual development support, and responsive problem-solving.

The Research on One-on-One Effectiveness

Research on management practices identifies regular one-on-one meetings as a high-impact activity for improving employee outcomes. Employees who have frequent, high-quality one-on-one conversations with their managers report significantly higher engagement, job satisfaction, and commitment to the organization (Heslin, Vandewalle, & Latham, 2006). Yet many managers treat one-on-ones as low priority, first things cancelled when calendars fill, or conducted irregularly only when "there's something to discuss."

Effective One-on-One Structure

Practitioner guidance such as from Tulgan (2017 & 2024) on effective one-on-ones suggests they should happen predictably (weekly or biweekly) and be protected from cancellation, focus primarily on employee needs rather than manager information gathering, address the person as a whole human rather than just a worker, include explicit development conversation beyond task updates, and result in action when issues are raised.

A simple structure can include:

- "How are you doing as a human being?" (personal check-in),
- "What obstacles can I remove for you?" (support needs)
- "How can I help you grow?" (development focus).

This structure signals that one-on-ones are support meetings, not status update meetings.

Community Building and Belonging: Creating Psychological Connection

Research in social psychology demonstrates that humans have fundamental needs for belonging and social connection that significantly influence happiness and wellbeing at work (Baumeister & Leary, 1995; Van den Broeck, Ferris, Chang, & Rosen, 2016).

Sense of Belonging Predicts Engagement

Research shows that employees who feel they belong, who have genuine relationships with colleagues, who feel valued by their team, who experience authentic connection, demonstrate significantly higher engagement and job satisfaction than those who feel isolated or marginally accepted (Cockshaw, Shochet, & Obst, 2013). Workplace belonging serves as a psychological resource that buffers stress, enhances wellbeing, and promotes organizational commitment (Van den Broeck, Ferris, Chang, & Rosen, 2016).

Managers influence belonging by:

- Creating opportunities for social interaction beyond task completion
- Modeling vulnerability and authenticity that makes others feel safe doing the same
- Noticing and addressing exclusion or clique formation
- Supporting employees through personal challenges
- Celebrating both work and personal milestones

Intentional Relationship Building

Strong teams don't develop accidentally. Deliberate practices can build team cohesion, including brief personal check-ins at meeting starts, team rituals that create shared identity, celebrations of both professional and personal milestones, and space for informal conversation alongside task focus. This can be especially important in remote or hybrid environments where casual hallway conversations don't happen naturally.

The Integration Challenge: Systematic Application

These practices aren't isolated techniques to be implemented separately. They're interconnected elements of a comprehensive approach to management that treats people as humans who happen to work rather than workers who happen to be human.

Recognition flows naturally from genuine observation and appreciation. Communication serves actual needs rather than checking boxes. Development happens through regular one-on-ones, not just annual reviews. Everything connects because it stems from the same source: genuine care for team wellbeing and success.

These practices work best when integrated as authentic expressions of genuine care for employee wellbeing rather than implemented as disconnected techniques or manipulative tactics (Avolio & Gardner, 2005). Employees readily distinguish between managers who genuinely value them and those merely following prescribed management behaviors.

The Requirements: What Makes This Work

Implementing these practices effectively requires several foundational commitments:

Consistency: Practices implemented sporadically provide little benefit. The power comes from consistent application over time.

Authenticity: Techniques used manipulatively destroy trust. These practices work when expressing genuine care, not when deployed as manipulation tools.

Personalization: While principles are universal, application must adapt to individual needs and preferences.

Patience: Engagement doesn't transform overnight. Sustained practice over months creates lasting change.

Accountability: Following through on commitments made during one-on-ones or in response to feedback. Without action, practices become empty exercises.

Conclusion: The Toolkit Exists

The practices that create employee happiness and engagement aren't mysterious. This chapter has identified them clearly:

- Model positive emotions and behaviors you want to see
- Recognize contributions specifically, timely, and authentically
- Communicate clearly, consistently, and honestly
- Help employees see meaning in their work
- Build trust through transparency and integrity
- Inspire through vision while investing in development
- Set clear goals collaboratively with regular feedback
- Maintain optimism while acknowledging reality
- Conduct regular one-on-ones focused on support
- Build community and belonging intentionally

None require exceptional personality, charisma, or resources. All require commitment, attention, and consistent practice. The toolkit exists. The research validates it. The question isn't whether these practices work, decades of evidence confirm they do. The question is whether managers will use them consistently and authentically.

Organizations that develop managers' capability and commitment to apply these practices create competitive advantages that compound over time. Those that leave management to individual interpretation achieve the predictably inconsistent results that 32.12% disengagement rates document.

The choice is clear: equip managers with evidence-based practices and hold them accountable for implementation or accept the consequences of systematic management failure. The toolkit is available. Will it be used?

Chapter 7

The Hidden Crisis: How Employee Disengagement Drains Global Profitability
(What Are the Effects on Profitability?)

I have explored why employee happiness matters, who's responsible for creating it, and how managers can foster it. Now comes the uncomfortable part: understanding exactly what we're losing when we fail. The numbers are so staggering they almost defy belief.

The Global Economic Catastrophe: $8.8 Trillion in Lost Value

Gallup (2023) indicated employee disengagement costs the global economy $8.8 trillion annually. Not billion with a B. Trillion with a T. According to research compiled by Gallup's State of the Global Workplace reports, this represents approximately 9% of global GDP, economic value that simply evaporates because people show up to work and operate at a fraction of their capability.

To put this in perspective, if employee disengagement were a country, it would have the third-largest GDP on Earth, behind only the United States and China. This $8.8 trillion is equivalent to the entire combined GDP of Japan and Germany, or roughly the total economic output of California, Texas, New York, and Florida combined.

This isn't money being poorly invested or inefficiently allocated. This is value that disappears into the void because hundreds of millions of workers worldwide are mentally checked out while physically present. It's like running every machine, every computer, every vehicle on the planet at 70% capacity, except worse, because disengaged humans don't just underperform; they actively create problems that engaged employees must then fix.

The mechanics of how disengagement destroys value exist in many forms. Disengaged employees make more errors that require correction. They provide worse customer service that drives clients away. They don't innovate or improve processes. They call in sick more frequently. They eventually quit, taking institutional knowledge with them. Each of these factors compounds the others, creating a cascade of value destruction.

Disengaged workers aren't just less productive, they can be harmful to organizational performance. They spread negativity that infects their co-workers. They resist change initiatives. They undermine leadership messages. They create friction that slows down teams. The cost isn't just what they don't produce; it's what they prevent others from producing.

When you aggregate these individual losses across billions of workers globally, you arrive at that almost incomprehensible $8.8 trillion figure that Gallup (2023) and others reference. And this estimate is conservative, it counts only direct productivity losses, not the full impact of innovation that never happened, relationships that soured, opportunities that vanished, or the compounding effects over time.

The Turnover Tsunami: Million-Dollar Hemorrhaging in Organizations

Let me make this more concrete by examining turnover costs, which represent one of the most measurable components of the disengagement crisis. Research by the Center for American Progress (Boushey and Glynn, 2012) shows that replacing an employee costs approximately 20% of annual salary for positions up to $50,000, and significantly more for specialized or executive roles.

For a 100-person organization with average salaries of $50,000 and a 30% annual turnover rate (near the industry average for many sectors), the math is brutal. Thirty employee departures per year, at $50,000 average salary, with typical replacement costs including:

- Recruitment costs: job board fees, recruiter commissions, interview time, background checks, approximately $15,000 per position
- Three months of lost productivity while the position sits vacant, $12,500 in lost output
- Training and onboarding for new hires, $8,000 for materials, time, and reduced productivity during ramp-up
- Six months of reduced productivity while the new hire reaches full performance, $25,000 in opportunity cost

- Knowledge loss and institutional memory gaps, $20,000 in inefficiencies and mistakes
  Impact on team morale and remaining employees' productivity, $7,000 in collateral damage

Total cost per departure: approximately $87,500. Multiply this by 30 annual departures, and you get $2.6 million, an amount that often exceeds the entire profit margin for organizations this size. Research by SHRM (Society for Human Resource Management) and Dyerly (2025) consistently finds that turnover costs range from 50% to 200% of annual salary depending on role complexity and seniority.

But these calculations only scratch the surface. When top performers leave, they often take key client relationships, institutional knowledge about systems and processes, and unique problem-solving capabilities that can't be easily replaced. High performer turnover creates cascading failures: remaining employees absorb additional workload, leading to increased stress and burnout, which drives further turnover in a downward spiral.

Studies such as Felps et al. (2009) show that turnover begets turnover. When valued colleagues leave, remaining employees reconsider their own commitment. When workload increases to fill gaps, work-life balance deteriorates. When institutional knowledge walks out the door, remaining employees struggle with problems that used to be easily solved. Each departure makes the next departure more likely.

The Absenteeism Drain: The Hidden Cost of Checking Out

While turnover represents permanent disengagement, absenteeism represents temporary but chronic disengagement. ActivTrak (2024) estimates disengaged workers cost their employers the equivalent of 18% of their annual salary through increased absenteeism alone. For a $50,000 employee, that's $9,000 annually in lost productivity.

Kaiser Permanente's 2022 research documented that disengaged workers take 38.08% more unplanned sick days than engaged employees. But the true cost extends far beyond the individual's absence. When a key employee calls in "sick" (whether due to actual illness or what researchers call "motivational absenteeism"), organizations face:

- Production disruptions as work either stops or must be redistributed
- Quality issues when less experienced substitutes fill critical roles
- Overtime costs for coverage
- Missed deadlines that trigger cascading failures in dependent projects
- Customer service failures when knowledgeable staff are absent

Research on burnout and absenteeism reveals a concerning pattern. Employees experiencing emotional exhaustion and burnout show significantly higher absence rates (Schaufeli, Bakker, & Van Rhenen, 2009). These absences often reflect psychological withdrawal rather than physical illness, employees whose emotional reserves are depleted find facing another workday unbearable. Job demands that exceed available resources predict both burnout and subsequent sickness absence, suggesting that many "sick days" actually represent mental health respite for psychologically exhausted workers.

Research demonstrates that absenteeism rates vary significantly across work units even when organizational policies, working conditions, and compensation are comparable, with management quality emerging as a key differentiating factor (Kuoppala, Lamminpää, Liira, & Vainio, 2008). Systematic reviews show that good leadership practices are associated with reduced sickness absence, while poor leadership predicts higher absence rates. The correlation is clear: toxic management drives absence, while supportive management reduces it, with absenteeism clustering predictably around management quality rather than organizational factors. The correlation is clear: toxic management drives absence, while supportive management reduces it. One department might have 8% unplanned absences while another has 2%, the only variable being leadership quality.

The Stress Epidemic: $300 Billion in Lost American Productivity

Job stress costs American companies more than $300 billion annually, according to research from the American Institute of Stress (2024) and data compiled by the University of

Massachusetts. This isn't just an economic statistic; it represents human suffering at scale.

Some of the components of stress-related costs according to American Institute of Stress (2022) include:

- Healthcare claims for stress-induced physical conditions, approximately $190 billion annually
- Stress-related workers' compensation claims, $24 billion
- Lost productivity from stress-impaired cognitive function, $63 billion
- Stress-driven turnover, $18 billion
- Absenteeism specifically attributable to stress, $12 billion

These numbers aggregate individual human experiences of chronic workplace stress. The physiological impact is well-documented: elevated cortisol levels that suppress immune function, increased cardiovascular risk from chronic fight-or-flight responses, sleep disruption that compounds cognitive impairment, gastrointestinal problems from sustained stress, and musculoskeletal disorders from sustained tension.

Research from Gallup's State of the Global Workplace Report (2022) identified the primary sources of employee burnout, with unfair treatment at work ranking as the single biggest driver. This is followed by unmanageable workloads, unclear communication from managers, lack of manager support, and unreasonable time pressure. Notably, all of these factors are directly controllable by organizational leadership, they aren't acts of nature but results of management choices.

The long-term health impacts of chronic workplace stress noted by the Occupational Safety and Health Administration (n.d.) include higher risk of cardiovascular disease, increased risk of Type 2 diabetes, increased gastrointestinal problems, chronic inflammation, and more musculoskeletal disorders. Organizations are literally shortening employees' lives through management practices that create chronic stress. If a factory were poisoning workers at these rates through chemical exposure, it would be shut down immediately. But because the poison is psychological, we've normalized it.

The Morale Crisis: Half a Trillion in Lost Potential

Clifford (2015) writes that poor employee morale costs American companies between $430-550 billion annually in lost productivity alone. This doesn't include turnover, healthcare, or customer losses, just the productivity hit from people who've emotionally checked out while physically present.

Imagine a professional sports team where players are giving 60% effort. They're still on the field, still going through the motions, but they're not really trying to win. Now imagine entire leagues playing this way. That's the American workforce, and research bears this out. Gallup's ongoing engagement research consistently finds that only about 30-35% of U.S. workers are actively engaged, meaning roughly two-thirds are either not engaged or actively disengaged. (Gallup, 2022)

Low morale manifests in observable organizational behaviors that research has documented. Employees stop voicing suggestions and concerns when they perceive their input is unwelcome or ignored, a withdrawal behavior that protects against repeated rejection (Detert & Burris, 2007). Disengagement spreads through social networks as newcomers are socialized into existing norms by veteran employees, a process that can rapidly convert enthusiastic new hires into cynical workers (Solinger et al., 2013). Employees experiencing chronic disengagement engage in psychological withdrawal, physically present but mentally disengaged, contributing only the minimum required to avoid negative consequences. These patterns create organizational cultures where initiative dies, participation becomes performative, and effort calibrates to bare minimums. This destruction of human potential should scandalize us. Organizations are paying people to be present while accepting that most of them are contributing a fraction of their capability. The waste isn't just economic; it's human. Millions of people spend 40+ hours weekly operating at a fraction of their potential, neither developing their capabilities nor contributing meaningfully to valuable outcomes. Unfortunately, I've been there myself. Getting told no over and over again when the initiative can help the company makes you question your ambitions at that company.

The Innovation Deficit: What Never Gets Created

Perhaps the most tragic aspect of the disengagement crisis isn't what we lose but what we never gain. Disengaged employees don't innovate, ever. Innovation requires risk-taking, creative thinking, and discretionary effort, none of which happen when people are emotionally absent.

Research on organizational innovation from Gallup (2023) consistently shows that companies with highly engaged workforces generate significantly more innovations, file more patents, and bring more new products to market. Gallup's research found that companies in the top quartile of engagement scores see:

- 10% higher customer ratings
- 14% higher productivity
- 18% higher sales
- 23% higher profitability
- 63% fewer safety incidents
- 78% lower absenteeism

The compound effect over time is staggering. Engaged organizations don't just perform better in any given quarter; they accelerate away from disengaged competitors until the gap becomes insurmountable. The initial advantage in innovation leads to better products, which attract more customers, which generate more resources for further innovation. Meanwhile, disengaged competitors stagnate, lose market position, and eventually fail or get acquired.

The Customer Experience Destruction

Employee disengagement doesn't stay internal, it bleeds into every customer interaction. Research including Gallup (2023) above consistently shows strong correlations between employee engagement and customer satisfaction scores. When employees are disengaged, they view customers as problems to be processed rather than people to be helped.

This manifests in countless small interactions that accumulate into terrible customer experiences: the retail worker who can't muster enthusiasm while helping a customer, the call center representative who mechanically follows scripts without actually solving problems, the service technician who does the minimum required work without taking pride in the result.

At my grandmother's funeral, the employee who was leading the prayer service at the funeral home began by asking everyone to join him in prayer and then he started "Bless us oh Lord, and these thy gifts…". He stopped – "Oh wait, no that's not it," he said. He began with a prayer that Catholics among others would typically say before they eat, not to begin a funeral service! The employee was checked out from the routine of his job; he was disengaged.

Each negative customer interaction doesn't just lose that sale; it destroys potential lifetime customer value. Research on customer lifetime value demonstrates that retaining customers generates substantially more value than acquiring new ones (Kumar & Reinartz, 2016). Loyal customers make repeated purchases, refer others, provide valuable feedback, and are less price-sensitive, creating compounding value over time that far exceeds their initial transaction. When disengaged employees create poor experiences, they're not just costing today's sale, they're eliminating years of future revenue.

Organizations track customer satisfaction metrics obsessively while often ignoring the employee engagement that drives those scores. The research is clear: fix employee engagement, and customer satisfaction follows. Ignore employee engagement, and no amount of customer service training or customer experience consulting will achieve lasting improvements.

The Competitive Disadvantage Multiplier

When one organization's workforce is disengaged while a competitor's is thriving, the disadvantaged organization faces an accelerating decline. The engaged competitor innovates while the disengaged stagnates. The engaged delights customers while the disengaged disappoints them. The engaged attracts top talent while the disengaged repels it.

This competitive disadvantage compounds over time. Initial market share losses make the disengaged organization less attractive to customers and employees. Resource constraints from declining performance limit ability to invest in improvements. Best performers leave for better opportunities, taking institutional knowledge and customer relationships. The organization enters a death spiral where each quarter's results are worse than the last.

The Opportunity Cost: What Could Have Been

As inferred from Gallup's (2023) report, perhaps the most profound tragedy of the $8.8 trillion disengagement crisis is understanding what that value could have created if it hadn't evaporated. If organizations could capture even half of the value currently lost to disengagement, the resources would be sufficient to make a major strive towards ending world hunger, provide clean water globally and advance healthcare, just to name a few things.

Instead, this value simply dissipates like heat radiating into space because we've created workplaces that transform human potential into human waste. The waste isn't just organizational; it's civilizational. We're squandering human capability on a scale that future generations will struggle to comprehend.

The Path Forward: From Loss to Gain

Consider the theoretical impact if global employee engagement increased by just 10 percentage points. Given that current disengagement costs an estimated $8.8 trillion annually, proportional improvements could yield trillions in economic value alongside substantial improvements in healthcare costs, innovation capacity, quality of life, and poverty reduction. While precise projections require complex modeling, the directional impact is clear: engagement improvements at scale would transform both economic and human outcomes.

Research suggests relationships between national wellbeing measures and economic outcomes. Countries with higher employee satisfaction and engagement tend to show stronger economic performance, though establishing clear causation remains complex due to numerous interconnected factors (Diener & Seligman, 2004). The pattern suggests that nations prioritizing human wellbeing, including workplace satisfaction, create conditions that support both economic prosperity and quality of life.

The path forward isn't mysterious. We know from research what creates engagement: meaningful work that connects to purpose, competent and supportive management, fair treatment that builds trust, opportunities for growth and development, and basic human respect. The research has been done. The evidence is overwhelming. The practices are well-documented.

The mystery isn't how to fix employee engagement. It's why, knowing all of this, we continue accepting the $8.8 trillion annual catastrophe of disengagement. The answer lies in organizational inertia, outdated mental models that treat employees as costs rather than investments, and management practices that prioritize short-term extraction of value over long-term creation of value.

Among the great economic opportunities of the 21st century including artificial intelligence, biotechnology, and space exploration, is solving the human engagement crisis. The technology and knowledge to do this already exists. What's missing is the organizational will to act and the leadership courage to prioritize human flourishing as a path to organizational success.

The $8.8 trillion question isn't whether we can afford to fix employee engagement. It's whether we can afford not to. Every day we delay represents another $24 billion evaporating into the void of human potential unrealized, another day where millions of people spend their working hours in misery rather than meaning, another day where organizations hemorrhage value they could be creating.

The crisis is real. The costs are quantified. The solutions are known. The only question remaining is whether we'll have the courage to act on what the research has been telling us for decades: that human happiness at work isn't a luxury or a distraction from business success, it's the foundation upon which all sustainable business success is built.

Chapter 8

The Biblical Mandate of Encouragement in Leadership and Employee Happiness
(The Heart of Encouraging Leadership)

The previous chapters have established through research and data that employee happiness drives organizational success. Now I want to turn to an ancient source of wisdom that has been instructing leaders for millennia: Scripture. The biblical mandate for encouragement in leadership isn't just spiritual guidance, it's remarkably practical wisdom for creating workplaces where humans thrive.

What's striking about biblical principles of leadership is how closely they align with modern research on organizational psychology and employee engagement. The ancient wisdom and contemporary research converge on the same fundamental truths about human motivation, dignity, and flourishing. This chapter explores how biblical teachings on encouragement provide a framework for leadership that builds both people and organizational success.

1 Thessalonians 5:11 – Building People, Not Just Processes

"Therefore encourage one another and build one another up, just as you are doing." NIV®

This verse captures something profound about human interaction: encouragement isn't optional or supplementary to leadership, it's central to it. The construction metaphor of "building one another up" reveals an important truth validated by modern psychology: in every interaction, leaders are either adding to people's confidence and capability or removing from it. There's no neutral ground.

The building metaphor is instructive. In construction, you either place materials that strengthen the structure or remove materials that weaken it. Similarly, every management interaction either reinforces employee confidence, competence, and engagement or undermines them. Leaders who understand this approach every interaction as an opportunity to add value to people, not just extract work from them.

Research on psychological capital, the positive psychological state characterized by self-efficacy, optimism, hope, and resilience, demonstrates that these qualities can be developed through intentional leadership practices and organizational interventions (Luthans, Youssef, & Avolio, 2007). Encouragement that recognizes effort, acknowledges progress, and affirms capability helps build employees' psychological capital, which in turn predicts performance, satisfaction, and wellbeing. Leaders who consistently provide supportive feedback and recognize achievements contribute to developing the psychological resources employees need to thrive at work. When leaders consistently "place bricks" through specific encouragement, they literally construct psychological resources that enable higher performance.

The phrase "just as you are doing" suggests encouragement should be a consistent, ongoing practice, not an occasional event. This aligns with research on recognition effectiveness, which shows that frequent, timely recognition has far greater impact on engagement than infrequent formal recognition programs. Biblical wisdom anticipated findings that organizational psychology would validate millennia later.

Organizations that implement systematic encouragement practices, where managers intentionally build people up through specific, timely recognition of effort and character, report measurable improvements in engagement, retention, and performance. This isn't because the encouragement manipulates behavior but because it meets fundamental human needs for appreciation and affirmation.

Ephesians 4:29 – Words That Give Grace

"Let no corrupting talk come out of your mouths, but only such as is good for building up, as fits the occasion, that it may give grace to those who hear." NIV®

The concept of "corrupting talk" extends beyond obvious insults or profanity. In organizational contexts, corrupting talk includes sarcasm disguised as humor, criticism delivered without construction, silence when encouragement is needed, and any communication that degrades rather than develops.

Edmonson (1999) demonstrates that team performance suffers dramatically when members fear that speaking up will result in embarrassment, rejection, or punishment. Teams with high psychological safety, where people feel safe taking interpersonal risks, consistently outperform teams with low psychological safety according to Edmondson (1999). Biblical wisdom about words that "give grace" rather than corrupt creates the foundation for psychological safety millennia before researchers had terminology for the concept.

The instruction that words should be "good for building up, as fits the occasion" suggests situational wisdom, different circumstances require different types of communication, but all should serve the purpose of development rather than destruction. This aligns with research on situational leadership and the importance of tailoring communication to individual needs and circumstances.

Even correction and accountability, which are necessary aspects of leadership, can be delivered in ways that build rather than break. Research on effective feedback shows that correction framed as developmental, focused on improvement rather than judgment, maintains engagement while improving performance (Steelman, Levy, & Snell, 2004). The difference between "this work is unacceptable" and "let's work together to bring this up to standard" isn't just semantic; it's the difference between destroying motivation and building capacity. Feedback that emphasizes learning and development rather than personal criticism preserves psychological safety while still addressing performance gaps.

Organizations that train leaders in grace-filled communication, where even difficult messages are delivered with respect for human dignity, report lower turnover, higher engagement, and better performance outcomes. Employees who receive developmental feedback perform better than those who receive purely critical feedback, validating the biblical principle that words should give grace while still addressing reality.

Hebrews 10:24-25 – The Power of Collective Encouragement

"And let us consider how to stir up one another to love and good works, not neglecting to meet together, as is the habit of some, but encouraging one another, and all the more as you see the Day drawing near." NIV®

The phrase "consider how" suggests encouragement requires intentionality and planning, it doesn't happen accidentally. This aligns with research on organizational culture, which demonstrates that positive cultures must be deliberately designed and consistently maintained. Without intentional effort to create encouragement, organizational default culture tends toward criticism and problem-focus.

The instruction to "not neglect to meet together" recognizes something modern research on social connection confirms: humans need regular interaction to maintain relationships and build community. Organizations that prioritize bringing people together, not just for task completion but for genuine connection and mutual encouragement, create stronger cultures and higher engagement.

Research on team dynamics shows that teams with regular opportunities for celebration and mutual appreciation outperform teams that only gather to solve problems or review failures. When organizations create intentional space for "stirring up one another to love and good works", for recognizing contributions, celebrating character, and building each other up, performance improves across multiple dimensions.

The biblical wisdom here is foundational to findings from positive organizational scholarship, which demonstrates that organizations that amplify positive elements (strengths, successes, contributions) achieve better outcomes than organizations that focus primarily on fixing negatives (weaknesses, failures, gaps). Both are necessary, but the ratio matters. Research on interpersonal dynamics suggests that positive interactions should substantially outnumber negative ones to maintain relationship quality, with ratios around 5:1 found in successful relationships (Gottman, 1994). While this research focused on personal relationships rather than workplace teams, the principle applies: predominant negativity destroys motivation and engagement, while predominantly positive interactions (including appropriate correction) support performance. Pure positivity without accountability is ineffective, but the overall emotional tone must be positive for teams to thrive.

Organizations that implement regular "victory celebrations" or "wins meetings" - dedicated time to recognize progress and encourage one another, report improved morale and engagement. This isn't frivolous feel-good activity; it's strategic culture building based on biblical wisdom validated by organizational research.

Proverbs 25:11 – The Art of Timely Encouragement

"A word fitly spoken is like apples of gold in a setting of silver." NIV®

This proverb emphasizes that timing matters enormously in communication, the right word at the wrong time loses much of its power. Modern research on recognition effectiveness validates this ancient wisdom: encouragement delivered immediately after the achievement or behavior creates a much stronger impact than delayed recognition (Daniels, 1994). The timeliness of feedback affects both its motivational power and its effectiveness in reinforcing desired behaviors, with recognition losing impact as time passes between the performance and the acknowledgment.

The neuroscience of habit formation explains why timing matters. When recognition immediately follows behavior, the brain creates strong associations between the behavior and the reward. Delayed recognition requires conscious memory retrieval and provides minimal motivational boost. Again, the "half-life" of recognition impact drops dramatically after 48-72 hours.

Organizations often fail at timely encouragement by saving recognition for formal annual reviews or quarterly meetings. By then, the specific achievements that deserved recognition are distant memories, and the opportunity to reinforce behaviors and create emotional impact has passed. The gold is present, but the timing is wrong, so the setting fails to showcase the value.

Biblical wisdom about fitly spoken words suggests that great communication requires both good content (the gold) and appropriate context (the silver setting). Leaders who recognize this develop skills in noticing when specific encouragement is needed and delivering it promptly. They understand that encouragement offered too late feels hollow, while encouragement offered thoughtfully at the moment of need feels like a gift.

Effective recognition programs share common characteristics: timely delivery, specific content, authentic appreciation, and appropriate context. These elements combine to create recognition that actually motivates rather than feeling perfunctory. The biblical image of gold in silver captures this beautifully, valuable substance presented in worthy context creates something more beautiful than either element alone.

1 Thessalonians 5:14 – Encouraging the Fainthearted

"And we urge you, brothers, admonish the idle, encourage the fainthearted, help the weak, be patient with them all." NIV®

This verse provides a framework for differentiated leadership, recognizing that different people need different things at different times. The idle need admonishment (accountability). The fainthearted need encouragement (affirmation). The weak need help (support). And everyone needs patience (grace for the process of growth).

Modern leadership research on situational leadership and emotional intelligence validates this differentiated approach (Hersey & Blanchard, 1969; Goleman, 1998). Effective leaders diagnose what each person needs and provide it. Treating everyone identically, whether with universal criticism or universal praise, fails to serve anyone well.

This biblical wisdom challenges the one-size-fits-all approach to management that many organizations default to. It requires leaders to actually know their people well enough to understand what each person needs. The brilliant employee struggling with imposter syndrome doesn't need more challenging assignments; they need encouragement that builds confidence. The struggling new hire doesn't need criticism; they need help and training. The complacent veteran coasting on past success doesn't need more encouragement; they need accountability and challenge.

Studies on employee development demonstrate that interventions work best when matched to individual needs (Heslin, Vandewalle, & Latham, 2006). Some employees benefit most from stretch assignments that challenge them. Others need skill development through training. Still others need confidence-building through encouragement and small wins. Leaders who diagnose individual needs and provide differentiated support achieve better results than those who apply standardized approaches.

The instruction to "be patient with them all" acknowledges that growth takes time and setbacks are normal. Research on learning and development confirms that sustainable behavior change requires patience and persistence, with habit formation typically requiring consistent repetition over extended periods (Lally, Van Jaarsveld, Potts, & Wardle, 2010). Organizations that expect instant transformation typically achieve only superficial compliance rather than genuine development.

Organizations that train managers in differentiated leadership, assessing individual needs and providing tailored support, report improved employee development outcomes, higher retention of top talent, and better overall team performance. The biblical framework provides a simple but profound model: diagnose the need (idle, fainthearted, weak) and provide the appropriate response (admonish, encourage, help) with patience for the process.

Proverbs 12:25 – Lifting the Weight of Anxiety

"Anxiety in a man's heart weighs him down, but a good word makes him glad." NIV®

This proverb recognizes a psychological reality validated by modern research: anxiety impairs performance and wellbeing, while encouragement provides relief and renewed energy. Organizations where anxiety dominates, where people worry constantly about job security, performance evaluation, organizational changes, or their own adequacy, cannot achieve optimal performance regardless of talent or resources.

As previously written, research on workplace stress and its impact on performance demonstrates clear negative effects. Chronic anxiety impairs cognitive function, particularly higher-order thinking like creativity and problem-solving. Anxious employees make more errors, take longer to complete tasks, and experience greater difficulty with complex work. The physiological effects of sustained anxiety include elevated cortisol, reduced immune function, and increased health problems.

Yet many organizations inadvertently run on anxiety as a management strategy. Vague threats about "performance improvement plans," uncertain futures, constant criticism without affirmation, and cultures of blame all create chronic anxiety that weigh people down exactly as the proverb describes.

The second part of the proverb offers the remedy: "a good word makes him glad." This isn't toxic positivity or pretending problems don't exist, it's genuine acknowledgment, authentic encouragement, and appropriate reassurance. When leaders acknowledge legitimate concerns while providing honest perspective and affirming people's value, they lift the weight of anxiety that impairs performance.

Organizations that address rather than amplify employee anxiety, through transparent communication, authentic encouragement, fair treatment, and supportive management, achieve better outcomes across multiple dimensions. Employees freed from chronic anxiety direct their cognitive resources toward productive work rather than self-protection.

They take intelligent risks rather than playing it safe. They innovate rather than merely complying.

Research on psychological safety from Edmondson (1999) and its impact on team performance validates the biblical wisdom: when leaders lift anxiety through encouragement and create conditions where people feel psychologically safe, performance improves dramatically. Google's Project Aristotle research, which analyzed hundreds of teams to identify factors predicting high performance, found psychological safety was the single most important factor, more important than team composition, individual talent, or resources (Rozovsky, 2015). This internal study validated academic research on psychological safety (Edmondson, 1999), demonstrating its practical importance in real organizational settings.

The Practical Implementation: Creating Encouragement Infrastructure

Biblical principles of encouragement aren't just for individual practice; they can be embedded in organizational systems and structures. Organizations that take encouragement seriously create what might be called "encouragement infrastructure", systematic practices that ensure encouragement happens consistently rather than randomly.

This infrastructure includes:

Meeting Structures: Starting gatherings with recognition before moving to problems creates a psychological frame that balances acknowledgment with improvement. Research shows this ordering matters, beginning with criticism and ending with praise feels disappointing, while beginning with praise and then addressing challenges feels motivating.

Communication Norms: Establishing expectations that all feedback include both acknowledgment of strengths and guidance for improvement creates consistent developmental communication. When correction without encouragement is seen as incomplete rather than acceptable, communication quality improves system-wide.

Recognition Systems: Creating regular opportunities for peer-to-peer encouragement (not just top-down) distributes encouragement throughout the organization and builds community. My survey revealed recognition from peers was more effective than recognition from managers.

Leadership Training: Developing managers' capacity to encourage effectively, teaching specific skills in timely recognition, differentiated support, and grace-filled communication, ensures encouragement becomes a core competency rather than a personality-dependent variable.

Accountability Metrics: Including encouragement and team development in performance evaluations for managers signals that building people is as important as achieving business results. When managers are evaluated and rewarded for creating engaged, developing teams, behavior changes system-wide.

The Theological Business Case

The alignment between biblical principles of encouragement and modern organizational research isn't coincidental. Christian perspectives on work and leadership suggest that biblical wisdom, rooted in divine understanding of human nature, should align with findings about human flourishing (Keller & Alsdorf, 2012). As Scripture reflects divine wisdom about human design and flourishing, we should expect that following biblical principles produces outcomes consistent with human thriving. The research validates this expectation.

Organizations that embrace biblical principles of encouragement, whether explicitly acknowledging the source or simply applying the principles, consistently achieve better outcomes: higher engagement, lower turnover, stronger performance, better innovation, improved customer satisfaction, and more sustainable success. These aren't spiritual outcomes requiring faith to perceive; they're measurable business results documented across industries and cultures.

This doesn't mean biblical principles work as mechanical techniques divorced from genuine care for people. Manipulation disguised as encouragement fails because people detect insincerity. The biblical principles work because they align with how humans are designed to flourish. When leaders genuinely care about building people up, treat them with dignity, speak words that give grace, encourage the fainthearted, and lift the weight of anxiety, they're working with human nature rather than against it.

Organizations don't need to be religious to benefit from biblical wisdom about encouragement. These principles work because they're true, they accurately describe human needs and effective ways to meet those needs. Whether leaders credit Scripture, organizational psychology, or practical experience, the practices themselves produce similar outcomes because they address the same underlying human realities.

The Ongoing Journey

Implementing biblical principles of encouragement isn't a one-time initiative but an ongoing practice. Organizations must consistently choose to build people up rather than tear them down, to speak words that give grace rather than corrupt, to encourage the fainthearted while helping the weak and challenging the idle.

This requires persistent intentionality because organizational defaults tend toward problem-focus and criticism. Without deliberate effort to create encouragement, cultures drift toward negativity. Leaders must continually choose to apply biblical principles even when it feels inefficient or unnecessary.

The payoff, however, is profound. Organizations that master biblical principles of encouragement create cultures where people flourish. Employees feel valued, develop their capabilities, contribute enthusiastically, and build genuine relationships. These cultures attract talent, retain top performers, innovate consistently, and achieve sustainable success.

The biblical mandate for encouragement in leadership isn't just for faith communities; it's for anywhere humans gather to accomplish shared goals. Since people spend enormous portions of their lives at work, the quality of workplace relationships and culture profoundly affects overall life satisfaction and human flourishing.

Leaders face a choice: build people up or tear them down through their words and actions. Biblical wisdom instructs clearly: choose to build. Modern research validates clearly: building produces better outcomes. The question isn't whether encouragement works, millennia of human experience and decades of research confirm it does. The question is whether leaders will have the courage and discipline to consistently apply principles that may feel uncomfortable initially but produce flourishing ultimately.

The biblical mandate is clear. The research confirmation is extensive. The practical applications are documented. The choice, as always, belongs to leaders: will they create organizations characterized by encouragement that builds people up, or will they accept cultures that tear people down? There is no neutral ground, every interaction either builds or destroys. Choose wisely.

Chapter 9

What Is Preventing Leaders from Creating Happiness?
(The Paradox of Modern Leadership)

I have tried to establish to this point that employee happiness drives organizational success. I have documented the staggering costs of disengagement. As well, so far I have identified evidence-based practices that create happiness. Additionally, I have explored biblical principles that align with modern research. Yet despite all this knowledge, most organizations continue failing at creating workplace happiness. Why?

In some instances, you no doubt have experienced people being put into a leadership position simply because they were deemed as a "Yes man". The Vice President installs a leader who will do whatever the Vice President will tell him to do, for example. This isn't true leadership, it's manipulation. You see unqualified people put into positions simply because they know the hiring manager or perhaps because they are willing to take a dramatically less salary for the lure of a manager title. Again, this isn't leadership.

The paradox is striking: organizations increasingly claim to value employee wellbeing while simultaneously creating conditions that systematically destroy it. They spend millions on perks and benefits while maintaining management practices that undermine engagement. They talk about culture while incentivizing behaviors that poison it. Understanding what prevents leaders from creating happiness despite knowing its importance reveals systemic barriers that must be addressed.

This chapter examines the structural, cultural, and psychological obstacles that prevent well-intentioned leaders from creating the workplace happiness that everyone agrees is important. These aren't excuses for failure, they're diagnoses that point toward solutions. Recognizing barriers is the first step toward removing them.

Barrier 1: The "Soft" Perception Problem

The word "soft" functions as professional profanity in many business contexts. "Soft skills," "soft metrics," "soft approach" all code for "not serious business." And happiness? That's perceived as the softest of the soft, appropriate for HR posters and team-building retreats but not for boardroom strategy.

This perception persists despite overwhelming evidence to the contrary. Research consistently demonstrates that employee engagement predicts financial performance, customer satisfaction, innovation rates, and virtually every outcome organizations claim to value. Gallup's (2022) extensive research shows companies with highly engaged workforces substantially outperform competitors across multiple dimensions. Yet somehow, engagement remains relegated to the "nice-to-have" category rather than recognized as strategically essential.

The soft perception creates a self-fulfilling cycle. Because happiness is seen as non-essential, organizations don't measure it rigorously. Because they don't measure it, they can't demonstrate its impact. Because they can't demonstrate impact, it continues being seen as soft. Breaking this cycle requires recognizing that the "soft" aspects of organizational life often have the hardest impact on outcomes that matter.

Consider the paradox: organizations will spend millions on technology systems to improve efficiency by 3%, but won't invest in engagement initiatives that could improve performance dramatically. They'll obsess over operational metrics while ignoring the employee engagement that drives those metrics. They'll track every conceivable business indicator except the one that most predicts whether they'll achieve their business goals.

The solution requires reframing the conversation. Happiness isn't soft; it's foundational. It's not supplementary to business success; it's predictive of it. Organizations that treat engagement as a key performance indicator alongside financial metrics begin to manage it with the same rigor, and achieve corresponding results.

I was in a company-wide meeting once where employees were asked to place their vote on how satisfied they were with their workplace. As more employees arrived and voted, the score continued to take a downward spiral. The company then used the same leadership that had been in place for some time to lead a new initiative on improving workplace satisfaction. If leadership wasn't serious about the issue in the past, how effective do you think the new initiative would be (without a major perception change)?

Barrier 2: Measurement Inadequacy

Management thinkers have long emphasized the importance of measurement in organizational performance (Drucker, 1954), but this principle has been distorted into "if you can't measure it, it doesn't matter", a dangerous oversimplification that dismisses crucial but hard-to-quantify factors like trust, culture, and psychological safety.

This distortion is particularly damaging regarding workplace happiness, where many organizations either don't measure engagement or measure it so poorly that the data provides little useful guidance. If it is measured, the results are often now transparent.

The typical approach, annual engagement surveys that take 43 minutes to complete, ask 97 questions about everything, and generate results 8 weeks later, exemplifies measurement theater rather than meaningful assessment. By the time results arrive, circumstances have changed. The granularity is either too high (overwhelming detail) or too low (meaningless averages). Response rates are poor because employees doubt anything will change. Actions taken in response are generic rather than targeted.

I have taken an employee survey before that asked specifically what department I was in, how many years I had been there, and many more very specific questions that would clearly identify me in this "anonymous" survey.

What employee in their right mind would feel comfortable completing such a survey in a toxic work environment?

Effective measurement of workplace happiness looks fundamentally different:

Frequency: Weekly or monthly pulse checks rather than annual surveys capture real-time sentiment and allow rapid response to emerging issues.

Brevity: 3-5 targeted questions taking 2-3 minutes to complete achieve high response rates and provide actionable data.

Specificity: Breaking results down by team, manager, department, and demographic reveals patterns that organization-wide averages mask.

Action-orientation: Measurement designed to guide specific interventions rather than generate comprehensive reports produces better outcomes.

Continuous tracking: Treating engagement as an ongoing metric rather than an annual event enables monitoring trends and evaluating intervention effectiveness.

Organizations that implement rigorous engagement measurement discover patterns invisible in annual surveys. Engagement varies dramatically by manager within the same organization. Certain events (performance review seasons, organizational changes, busy seasons) predictably affect engagement. Some teams maintain high engagement despite challenging circumstances while others struggle despite advantages.

With real data, organizations can take real action. Instead of organization-wide initiatives that may or may not address actual issues, they can target specific problems: providing additional support to managers whose teams show low engagement, addressing specific concerns raised in particular departments, intervening when engagement dips suggest emerging problems.

Research organizations like Gallup (2022) and others have developed validated instruments and methodologies for measuring engagement. These aren't secret formulas requiring expensive consultants, they're proven approaches that any organization can implement. The barrier isn't lack of measurement tools; it's organizational will to measure rigorously and act on results. You can also use the same questions I have posed in this book for your team and compare those results to the national average as a guide.

Barrier 3: Misaligned Incentive Structures

Perhaps the most systemic barrier to creating workplace happiness is that organizational incentive structures consistently reward behaviors that destroy engagement while failing to reward behaviors that create it. You probably just thought of a person who was a terrible leader yet was given a new title, new responsibilities or higher status in the organization.

Managers who achieve short-term results by burning through teams get promoted. Managers who build sustainable, engaged teams but miss one quarterly target get put on performance improvement plans. The message is clear and consistently reinforced: results matter; how you achieve them doesn't.

This misalignment cascades throughout organizations. A manager who wants to invest in team development must justify the time away from immediate productive work. A leader who wants to have difficult but necessary conversations about workload must defend the impact on short-term deliverables. An executive who wants to refuse unrealistic commitments to protect team wellbeing faces pressure from boards focused on growth regardless of sustainability.

The problem isn't that results don't matter, obviously they do. The problem is treating results and engagement as a zero-sum tradeoff rather than recognizing that sustainable results require engaged teams. Organizations that sacrifice engagement for short-term results discover they've made a terrible trade: temporarily better numbers purchased with talent departure, increased errors, innovation decline, and eventual performance collapse.

Organizations serious about employee happiness must align incentives with desired outcomes in areas such as:

Evaluation criteria: Include team engagement, development, and retention in performance assessments for all managers, weighted significantly enough to affect advancement and compensation.

Promotion standards: Require demonstrated capability in building and leading engaged teams as a prerequisite for advancement into leadership roles, not just technical excellence or individual achievement.

Compensation models: Tie meaningful portions of leadership compensation to team engagement metrics, making the "soft" stuff financially material.

Recognition systems: Celebrate leaders who build engaged, sustainable teams as prominently as those who achieve exceptional short-term results.

Succession planning: Ensure that people advanced into leadership positions have demonstrated capacity for creating engagement, not just delivering results through any means necessary.

When promotions are done with these characteristics in mind, most employees will not be surprised when that specific person gets promoted or rewarded.

When organizations implement these changes, making engagement financially and professionally material for leaders, behavior changes remarkably quickly. Suddenly, the "soft" stuff becomes very hard currency. Managers who previously ignored engagement because it wasn't measured or rewarded begin paying attention when it affects their bonuses and career prospects.

Organizations that hold managers accountable for engagement through performance evaluations and compensation create powerful incentives for behavior change. Research demonstrates that what gets measured and rewarded gets prioritized (Kerr, 1995). The practices that create engagement aren't mysterious or difficult, they're well-documented in decades of research (Harter et al., 2020). Leaders simply need sufficient motivation to implement them consistently, and accountability systems provide that motivation.

Barrier 4: The Pressure Cascade

Middle managers face an impossible bind: pressure from above to deliver results at any cost and expectations from below to create positive, supportive environments. When these forces conflict, and they inevitably do, guess which one wins?

Senior leaders give speeches about work-life balance while sending emails at midnight, on Saturdays during the kids' soccer game or worse on Sunday during your last refuge of rest. They talk about psychological safety as described by Edmondson (1999) while punishing failures. They preach empowerment while micromanaging decisions. They mandate culture change while maintaining systems that reward opposite behaviors.

This schizophrenia cascades down organizational hierarchies. Middle managers become transmission belts of dysfunction, passing along pressure while having neither authority to change systems creating the pressure nor freedom to shield their teams from it. They're held accountable for employee engagement while being denied resources and authority necessary to create it.

The structural problem is that organizations typically optimize for short-term extraction of value rather than long-term creation of value. Projects are scoped assuming people will work excessive hours. Timelines are set assuming no unexpected problems arise. Resources are allocated assuming perfect efficiency. When reality doesn't match these assumptions, and it never does, the slack gets absorbed by people working harder, longer, and less sustainably. As I write this, I am remembering a past co-worker of mine who had a tremendous amount of work put on him to the point you could visibly see the stress in him every day. He was miserable and his health suffered from it.

Solving this requires confronting uncomfortable realities about capacity, timelines, and sustainability. It requires saying no to opportunities that would require burning through teams. It requires building slack into systems rather than optimizing for theoretical maximum output. It requires accepting that sustainable high performance looks different from sprinting until people collapse.

Organizations that empower middle managers to push back on unrealistic expectations, that treat sustainable pace as a constraint rather than a nice-to-have, create conditions where engagement becomes possible. Those that continue squeezing maximum short-term output regardless of sustainability create conditions where engagement becomes impossible regardless of management skill.

Barrier 5: Emotional Leadership Discomfort

Many leaders, particularly those who advanced through technical or financial expertise, are profoundly uncomfortable with emotional leadership. They prefer spreadsheet analysis to feelings, technical problem-solving to human complications. This discomfort manifests as avoidance of the very interactions that create engagement.

Leaders who avoid one-on-ones, who give feedback only through email, who address emotional situations with logic and data, who never ask about people's lives beyond work, these leaders aren't necessarily uncaring. Often, they're anxious about saying the wrong thing, appearing weak, or not knowing how to help. They'd rather say nothing than risk making situations worse through clumsy intervention.

This avoidance creates distance that employees interpret as lack of caring. When leaders never ask, "how are you doing?" and actually listen to the answer, employees conclude their wellbeing doesn't matter. When leaders avoid difficult conversations, problems fester. When leaders hide behind professional distance, they sacrifice the human connection that engagement requires.

The solution isn't transforming introverted engineers, for example, into charismatic motivational speakers. It's developing basic competencies in emotional intelligence and human connection. Simple practices like asking about people's lives, acknowledging when someone seems stressed, saying "that must be difficult" when someone shares a challenge, these aren't complex emotional interventions.

They're basic human decency that creates psychological safety and connection. If you are such an introvert leader, I implore you to be transparent with your team about it! They will thank you for acknowledging it and you will most likely have one of your team members volunteer to help you with the personal aspect of your job.

Organizations can develop leaders' capacity for emotional leadership through training, coaching, modeling, and practice. The skills can be learned. The discomfort can be overcome. But it requires recognizing emotional leadership as a developable competency rather than an innate personality trait some people have and others don't.

Research shows that emotional intelligence can be systematically developed through training and practice (Mattingly & Kraiger, 2019). Leaders who commit to building these capabilities, who practice having authentic conversations, who learn to recognize and respond to emotional cues, who develop comfort with vulnerability, achieve better results with their teams. The discomfort doesn't disappear entirely, but competence grows and avoidance decreases as leaders develop greater emotional awareness and interpersonal skills.

Barrier 6: Leader Burnout and Self-Neglect

Perhaps the darkest truth about leadership failure to create happiness is that many leaders are themselves so depleted they have nothing left to give. You can't pour from an empty cup, and many leadership cups have been empty for years.

Leaders working 70+ hour weeks, taking no real vacations, sacrificing family relationships, neglecting health, taking medication just to function, these leaders are expected to inspire teams, create energy, and care about others' development while barely managing their own survival. The expectation is unrealistic and the results are predictable: exhausted leaders create exhausted teams.

Organizations often create this problem through the way they promote and support leaders. They advance people into leadership based on individual contribution, provide minimal training and support, establish impossible expectations, and then wonder why leaders struggle. They demand more from leaders while providing less, creating conditions where burnout becomes almost inevitable.

The systemic nature of this problem means individual solutions, better time management, stress reduction techniques, self-care practices, address symptoms without fixing root causes. Leaders need organizational support: realistic workload expectations, genuine authority matching responsibility, development resources, peer support systems, and explicit permission to maintain healthy boundaries.

Research on leader wellbeing and team performance demonstrates clear connections (Barling & Cloutier, 2017; Harms, Credé, Tynan, Leon, & Jeung, 2017). Burned-out leaders create disengaged teams through emotional contagion and diminished leadership capacity.

I remember seeing a past leader of mine throw binders against the wall and sit at his desk with his hands over his face repeatedly saying "I can't do this anymore; I can't do it!" Within three years, six of the eight members in our group left the company.

Leaders who model sustainable work practices build more engaged and productive teams. Organizations that support leader wellbeing achieve better overall results than those that grind leaders down, as leader stress and exhaustion cascade to team members and undermine collective performance.

Addressing leader burnout requires systemic changes: examining workload realities, providing adequate staffing and resources, clarifying decision authority, creating peer support networks, modeling sustainable practices from senior leadership, and treating leader wellbeing as organizationally important rather than individually managed.

Barrier 7: Cultural Norms Equating Suffering with Dedication

Many organizations maintain cultural norms that equate suffering with dedication: the person working weekends is committed; the person maintaining boundaries isn't a team player. The manager responding to emails at 2 AM shows dedication; the one who disconnects shows lack of commitment. These norms poison efforts to create workplace happiness by making misery a badge of honor.

These norms are often unwritten but powerfully enforced through social pressure and modeling. Senior leaders who brag about not taking vacation signal that vacation is weakness. Managers who celebrate all-nighters signal that work-life balance is for slackers. Organizations that promote the person who sacrificed everything signal that sacrifice is the path to advancement.

Changing cultural norms requires deliberate effort and consistent modeling from leadership. It requires calling out the valorization of suffering and reframing it as unsustainable. It requires celebrating leaders who achieve results sustainably rather than those who burn brightest before flaming out. It requires explicitly stating that boundaries are healthy and expected rather than signs of limited commitment.

Organizations that successfully shift these norms report better retention, higher engagement, and often better performance (Haar, Russo, Suñe, & Ollier-Malaterre, 2014). Sustainable high performance consistently outperforms unsustainable sprints over time, as recovery and renewal enable sustained productivity (Fritz & Sonnentag, 2006). The cultural shift isn't easy, norms are deeply embedded and resistant to change, but it's possible with persistent effort and consistent modeling.

Barrier 8: The Fundamental Misunderstanding of Happiness

Many leaders genuinely want to create workplace happiness but fundamentally misunderstand what it is. They think happiness equals fun, so they install game rooms. They think it means easy, so they lower standards. They think it means constant positivity, so they ban difficult conversations.

Real workplace happiness isn't about ping-pong tables or casual Fridays. It's about meaningful work connected to purpose, growth opportunities that challenge and develop, respect that acknowledges human dignity, fairness that builds trust, achievement that creates pride, relationships that provide support, autonomy that enables ownership, and recognition that validates contribution.

None of these require expensive perks. All require genuine leadership commitment and skillful execution. Organizations that understand this achieve engagement without massive budgets. Those that misunderstand it waste money on surface improvements while leaving fundamental problems unaddressed.

The solution requires education about what actually creates workplace happiness. Research presented thus far make it clear on the factors that matter: psychological safety, meaningful work, supportive management, fair treatment, growth opportunities, authentic recognition, and human connection. These aren't mysterious or complex, but they're also not achieved through perks and amenities.

Organizations serious about employee happiness study the research, understand the factors that actually drive engagement, and implement evidence-based practices. They stop confusing happiness with fun and recognize it as a serious business strategy requiring serious implementation.

The Systems Problem: Integration and Interdependence

Individual barriers are challenging enough, but the real difficulty comes from their interaction. Organizations maintain incentive structures that reward destructive behaviors while their culture valorizes suffering, while their leaders are burned out and emotionally disconnected, while their measurement systems provide no useful data, while happiness is perceived as soft. Each barrier reinforces others, creating systems that resist change even when individual leaders sincerely want to improve.

Addressing this systems problem requires coordinated action across multiple dimensions:

Reframing the narrative: Treating engagement as strategically essential rather than culturally soft, backed by rigorous measurement demonstrating impact.

Realigning incentives: Making engagement financially and professionally material through evaluation criteria, compensation models, and advancement requirements.

Supporting leaders: Providing realistic expectations, adequate resources, genuine authority, development opportunities, and peer support.

Changing cultural norms: Explicitly rejecting suffering-as-dedication mindset and celebrating sustainable high performance.

Developing competencies: Building leaders' capabilities in emotional intelligence, developmental conversation, and engagement practices.

Measuring rigorously: Implementing real-time, actionable engagement measurement that guides targeted interventions.

The good news is that these elements reinforce each other positively just as they currently reinforce each other negatively. As measurement improves, impact becomes visible. As impact becomes visible, perception shifts from soft to strategic. As perception shifts, incentives begin aligning. As incentives align, leadership behavior changes. As behavior changes, culture evolves. As culture evolves, engagement improves. As engagement improves, results validate the approach.

Organizations that commit to comprehensive, systemic approaches to creating workplace happiness, addressing multiple barriers simultaneously rather than hoping individual initiatives will overcome systemic obstacles, achieve transformation. Those that continue making small changes while leaving fundamental systems intact achieve minimal progress.

The Path Forward

Understanding what prevents leaders from creating happiness despite knowing its importance provides a roadmap for action. The barriers are real but not insurmountable. They're systemic but not permanent. They're deeply embedded but not unchangeable.

Organizations that successfully remove these barriers share common characteristics: senior leadership commitment extending beyond rhetoric to resource allocation and personal modeling, systemic approach addressing multiple barriers simultaneously, rigorous measurement enabling data-driven improvement, and persistence through initial resistance and setbacks.

The question isn't whether these barriers can be overcome, organizations around the world demonstrate daily that they can. The question is whether your organization will commit to overcoming them, with all the discomfort, investment, and change that requires. Because make no mistake: creating genuine workplace happiness in organizations currently structured to prevent it requires real change, not superficial initiatives.

The choice is clear: continue accepting the barriers and their consequences, or commit to removing them and achieving the results that research promises and exemplar organizations demonstrate. The barriers are real. But so are the solutions, and so are the results for organizations courageous enough to act.

Chapter 10

The Ripple Effect of Happiness at Work

Introduction: Beyond the Paycheck

Throughout this book, I have examined workplace happiness primarily through an organizational lens, exploring its impact on productivity, profitability, retention, and business success. But workplace happiness doesn't stay contained within office walls. It radiates outward, affecting families, communities, and society in ways that extend far beyond quarterly earnings reports.

This chapter explores the ripple effects of workplace happiness, documenting how what happens during working hours can affect everything from family dynamics to civic engagement to public health to democratic stability. The research reveals that workplace happiness isn't just an organizational concern, it's a societal imperative with implications that touch nearly every aspect of human flourishing.

Understanding these broader impacts reframes the conversation about workplace happiness from a business strategy discussion to a human flourishing imperative. When we recognize that workplace misery creates collateral damage extending across families and communities, the cost-benefit calculation shifts dramatically. When we understand that workplace happiness creates beneficial ripples that strengthen society, the investment becomes not just justified but essential.

The Personal Ripple: Individual Health and Wellbeing

Mental and Emotional Health

The relationship between workplace conditions and mental health is well established in psychological and medical research. Chronic workplace stress is a significant contributor to depression, anxiety disorders, and related mental health conditions, while positive workplace experiences and happiness are consistently associated with improved psychological well-being and overall mental health outcomes (Harvey et al., 2017; Warr, 2007; World Health Organization, 2022).

Work matters far more to our mental health than most people realize. Research has long shown that job satisfaction is one of the strongest predictors of overall life satisfaction, second only to our closest personal relationships (Warr, 2007). That makes sense when you consider how much time we spend at work, often more waking hours with coworkers than with the people we love most (Gallup, Inc., 2023). When those hours are filled with pressure, frustration, and a sense that nothing we do really matters, the emotional weight adds up (Harvey et al., 2017).

Over time, unhealthy work environments begin to leave visible marks. People in chronically stressful jobs experience much higher rates of depression and anxiety than those in supportive workplaces (Harvey et al., 2017). This isn't just coincidence. When people move from toxic environments into healthier ones, their mental health often improves. When they move the other direction, it often declines. Work doesn't just reflect how people feel, it actively shapes it (Warr, 2007).

The reason is simple: work touches many of our deepest psychological needs at once. Meaningful work gives people a sense of purpose. Supportive colleagues and managers create connection and belonging. Fair treatment affirms dignity and self-worth. Recognition and achievement build confidence. Psychological safety reduces the constant background stress that slowly drains emotional energy (World Health Organization, 2022). When these elements are missing, people don't just feel dissatisfied, they feel depleted.

Mental health professionals see this reality every day. Workplace stress is one of the most common factors behind the anxiety, burnout, and depression they treat (World Health Organization, 2022). Many patients don't need new medications or complex interventions as much as they need better work conditions. In fact, some clinicians can predict when demand will spike simply by looking at organizational calendars, performance reviews, restructuring announcements, and high-pressure deadlines reliably send more people looking for help (Harvey et al., 2017).

Work, in other words, is not a neutral backdrop to life. It is one of its most powerful emotional environments. When work is healthy, it supports mental well-being. When it isn't, the cost shows up quietly but persistently, in people's minds, relationships, and lives.

Physical Health

The body keeps score of workplace conditions through measurable physiological effects. Research in occupational health and psychosomatic medicine documents extensive physical health impacts of workplace stress versus workplace happiness.

Chronic work-related stress creates sustained elevation in cortisol and other stress hormones, which over time suppress immune function, increase inflammation, disrupt sleep, elevate blood pressure, and contribute to metabolic dysfunction (McEwen, 2007; Cohen et al., 2012). The cumulative effect manifests in measurably worse health outcomes as previously mentioned (American Institute of Stress, 2022).

Research measuring biological markers of aging demonstrates that workplace conditions affect health at the cellular level. Studies of telomere length, the protective caps on chromosomes that indicate biological age, show that employees in toxic work environments have shorter telomeres consistent with accelerated aging (Epel et al., 2004; Puterman et al., 2016). Happy employees show telomeres typical of people many years younger than their chronological age (Puterman et al., 2016). The implication is stark: workplace misery is literally aging people faster.

The mechanism involves chronic activation of stress response systems. Human bodies evolved to handle acute stressors followed by recovery periods. Modern workplace stress often creates chronic activation without adequate recovery, leading to system dysregulation. Saturday and Sunday simply are not enough when most of Sunday is dreading experiencing the stress all over again in the upcoming week.

Healthcare utilization patterns reflect workplace impact. Employees in high-stress roles use healthcare services more frequently, file more workers' compensation claims, require more mental health treatment, and consume more medications (Dewa et al., 2014; Goetzel et al., 2018). The economic costs of workplace-induced health problems run into the hundreds of billions of dollars annually in the United States alone (American Institute of Stress, 2022; Goh et al., 2016).

Conversely, workplace happiness creates measurable health benefits. Research documents lower blood pressure, better immune function, improved sleep quality, healthier weight, and reduced need for both physical and mental health interventions among employees in supportive work environments. The health dividend of workplace happiness isn't small, it's substantial and measurable.

Purpose, Identity, and Self-Worth

Humans are meaning-making creatures. We need to feel that our existence matters, that we're contributing to something beyond ourselves. For many adults, work represents the primary context where this meaning gets sought and either found or frustrated.

Research on meaning and purpose in life consistently identifies work as one of the most important domains where people seek significance. According to Pew Research Center (2021) studies, work ranks second only to family and children as a source of life meaning for most adults. When employees find their work meaningful, they experience increased job satisfaction, higher engagement, and stronger sense of organizational loyalty.

The psychological impact of meaningful versus meaningless work extends far beyond job satisfaction. People who experience their work as meaningful consistently report higher life satisfaction, stronger mental health, a clearer sense of purpose, and greater resilience when facing life's challenges. In contrast, individuals who perceive their work as meaningless or misaligned with their values show lower levels of well-being, even when other aspects of their lives are stable or positive (Steger et al., 2012; Wrzesniewski et al., 1997).

This dynamic helps explain why people sometimes accept lower pay for work they find meaningful while rejecting higher-paying work that feels meaningless. **The psychological value of meaningful work exceeds its monetary value. Conversely, no amount of compensation fully compensates for work that violates values or feels purposeless.**

The ripple effect operates through identity formation. Work shapes how people see themselves and how they're seen by others. When work affirms human dignity and allows contribution to valued outcomes, it builds positive self-concept and healthy identity. When work dehumanizes or produces outcomes that create moral distress, it damages self-concept and fragments identity.

Research on moral injury, psychological harm from participating in or witnessing actions that violate deeply held moral beliefs, originally focused on combat veterans but increasingly applies to workplace contexts. Employees who feel their work contradicts their values or harms others experience forms of moral distress that affect overall wellbeing beyond work hours.

The Familial Ripple: Stronger Families and Relationships

Energy and Presence

Perhaps the most immediate and visible ripple effect of workplace happiness flows into family relationships through the energy and emotional presence people bring home. Decades of research on the work–family interface show that workplace conditions do not stay contained at work; they spill over into family life in predictable ways, shaping daily interactions, emotional availability, and relationship quality (Greenhaus & Beutell, 1985; Frone, 2003).

Employees who leave work energized and fulfilled bring that positivity home. Studies on work–family facilitation indicate that these employees tend to have greater patience for family members' concerns, more energy for maintaining relationships, and more emotional capacity for handling family challenges (Voydanoff, 2004). Their attention is more present in the small moments that build family bonds, creating a healthier emotional climate at home.

Conversely, employees depleted by workplace stress arrive home exhausted. Research on work–family conflict consistently finds that stress carried from work reduces patience for minor frustrations, diminishes engagement in family activities, and limits emotional resources for relationship challenges (Frone, 2003). Even when people deeply care about their families, workplace misery can cast long shadows across family life.

This pattern shows up clearly in relationship outcomes. Marital satisfaction, for example, correlates significantly with job satisfaction, not because happy people are simply happy everywhere, but because workplace stress and fulfillment directly affect the capacity required for relationship maintenance (Amstad et al., 2011). Parenting quality follows similar trends. Studies of working parents show that chronic workplace stress is associated with lower patience, reduced engagement, and decreased emotional availability with children (Crouter et al., 2001).

Longitudinal research following families through employment changes reinforces these findings. When a parent moves from a toxic workplace to a supportive one, family members report improvements in relationship quality, household atmosphere, and overall family functioning. When the transition moves in the opposite direction, family dynamics deteriorate in measurable ways (Voydanoff, 2004; Amstad et al., 2011). These shifts underscore that workplace conditions actively shape family systems over time.

The mechanism operates through both time and quality dimensions. Workplace stress often demands longer hours, leaving less time available for family life, a dynamic identified early in work–family conflict theory (Greenhaus & Beutell, 1985). But beyond time, stress degrades the quality of time together. Research shows that physical presence without emotional availability leaves family members feeling disconnected even when they are together (Frone, 2003). The parent scrolling through work email during dinner may be present in body but absent in attention.

Parenting research makes this impact especially clear. Even after controlling for factors such as income, education, and personality, workplace conditions independently predict parenting behaviors. Parents in supportive work environments demonstrate more warmth, involvement, consistent discipline, and emotional attunement than parents in high-stress roles (Crouter et al., 2001). In this way, workplace happiness quietly shapes not only employees' lives but also the emotional experiences of the next generation.

Modeling and Values Transmission

Children learn about work, career, success, and life priorities not primarily from what parents say but from what they observe and experience. Parents' relationships with their work become implicit lessons about what working life means and what success costs. I can remember as a child I always said I was going to work smarter rather than harder as I watched the effects of working the night shift on my father and our family.

When children observe parents who dread work, who arrive home depleted, who sacrifice family for career demands, who experience work as necessary suffering, children internalize these lessons. They develop expectations that working life requires misery, that success demands sacrifice of wellbeing, that pursuing meaning in work is naive or impractical.

Conversely, when children observe parents who find fulfillment in work, who maintain healthy boundaries, who integrate career and family successfully, who experience work as meaningful contribution, children internalize very different lessons. They develop beliefs that fulfilling work is possible, that success doesn't require sacrificing wellbeing, that pursuing meaning in career is legitimate and achievable.

Research on occupational socialization suggests that parental work experiences influence children's attitudes toward work and career development (Johnson & Mortimer, 2011). Parents' satisfaction and experiences at work shape the messages children receive about employment, careers, and workplace expectations. When parents model positive work experiences and discuss work in affirming ways, children develop different career attitudes than when parents consistently express frustration, cynicism, or dissatisfaction with their work lives.

The intergenerational transmission of these patterns creates cycles that can be either virtuous or vicious. Workplace happiness or misery ripples not just across one generation but potentially across multiple generations through the lessons about work that children internalize.

Economic Stability and Opportunity

Workplace happiness affects families economically through multiple channels beyond direct compensation. Research demonstrates that happy, engaged employees earn more over career lifespans, experience less involuntary job loss, achieve more career advancement, and build more stable economic foundations for families (Lyubomirsky, King, & Diener, 2005).

Engaged employees develop skills more rapidly, build stronger professional networks, generate more opportunities, and achieve better career outcomes. These advantages compound over time, creating significant economic differences in lifetime earnings. Research tracking career trajectories shows that early-career engagement predicts long-term economic outcomes even after controlling for initial education and ability (Judge, Thoresen, Bono, & Patton, 2001).

The stability dimension matters as much as absolute income level. Families dealing with chronic job insecurity or frequent involuntary transitions face ongoing stress regardless of income level. Workplace happiness contributes to employment stability, which provides economic and psychological benefits beyond what income alone captures (De Witte, Pienaar, & De Cuyper, 2016).

Research on economic mobility shows that family economic stability during childhood strongly predicts children's future outcomes (Chetty, Hendren, Kline, & Saez, 2014). When parents experience workplace stability and satisfaction, children benefit not just from immediate economic security but from reduced household stress, more consistent parenting, and better developmental environments.

The Community Ripple: Civic Engagement and Social Capital

Civic Participation

Happy employees don't just go home and recover from work, they have energy remaining to contribute to communities. Research on civic engagement demonstrates connections between workplace satisfaction and community participation (Sonnentag, Mojza, Binnewies, & Scholl, 2008).

Research suggests that employees in satisfying work environments participate more actively in community life, volunteering at higher rates, participating in local governance more frequently, and engaging in community improvement projects more often (Rodell, 2013). Work experiences that deplete energy and create chronic stress leave people with fewer resources for civic contribution, while positive work experiences that energize and engage create capacity for broader community involvement.

The mechanism is straightforward: civic engagement requires time, energy, and emotional resources. Workplace misery depletes these resources, leaving little for community contribution. Workplace happiness preserves or even creates surplus resources that flow into community engagement.

Research on social capital and community wellbeing suggests relationships between employment conditions and civic participation. Studies examining the impact of job loss on communities demonstrate that unemployment reduces civic engagement and weakens community ties (Brand, 2015). This suggests that employment experiences, not just employment status, may influence capacity for community participation. Areas where residents experience positive workplace conditions would be expected to show higher civic participation rates, stronger community organizations, and greater social capital, as workers have energy and resources remaining for community contribution rather than arriving home depleted from unsatisfying work. The implications are significant. Strong communities require engaged citizens willing to contribute time and energy to collective needs. When workplaces drain people, communities suffer from reduced civic capacity. When workplaces energize people, communities benefit from surplus engagement.

Social Capital and Community Cohesion

Social capital, the networks, relationships, norms, and trust that enable cooperation and collective action, requires ongoing investment of time and attention. Workplace happiness versus misery affects people's capacity and willingness to make these investments.

Research on work-life spillover demonstrates that workplace stress depletes psychological resources needed for social participation outside work (Ten Brummelhuis & Bakker, 2012). Daily workload and negative workplace experiences reduce employees' capacity for social behaviors and relationship building in non-work domains (Ilies et al., 2007). Community relationship building requires energy that workplace-stressed individuals lack, as work demands consume the psychological resources, time, attention, emotional capacity, that social capital formation requires.

Happy employees are more likely to know neighbors, participate in local social networks, contribute to community events, and build the relationships that constitute social capital.

Robert Putnam's research on social capital decline in America, documented in Bowling Alone (2000), identified multiple contributing factors including television, suburban sprawl, and generational change. While he didn't focus specifically on workplace satisfaction, subsequent research suggests that increasing workplace stress and deteriorating job quality contribute to social capital erosion by reducing people's capacity for community engagement.

The community-level effects extend beyond individual participation to many outcomes. Communities with higher concentrations of workplace-satisfied residents show better social cohesion, lower crime rates, stronger local institutions, more effective community problem-solving, and generally higher quality of life. The mechanisms involve both individual contribution and collective atmosphere, communities composed of energized, engaged residents function better than communities of depleted, withdrawn residents.

The Societal Ripple: Public Health and Democratic Stability

Public Health Impact

If workplace happiness or misery affects individual health as documented earlier, aggregating these effects across populations creates public health implications. Research modeling the population-level health impacts of improved workplace conditions suggests massive potential benefits.

Research demonstrates that workplace stressors contribute substantially to adverse health outcomes including increased mortality risk, elevated healthcare costs, mental health disorders, and substance abuse (Goh, Pfeffer, & Zenios, 2016). Workplace conditions, including job demands, work-family conflict, shift work, and job insecurity, are associated with increased risk of physician-diagnosed illness and premature mortality. While precise estimates of potential improvements from addressing workplace stress vary depending on modeling assumptions, the evidence clearly indicates that workplace conditions represent a significant, modifiable determinant of population health outcomes.

The mechanism operates through both direct effects on health behaviors and indirect effects through mental health. Workplace stress contributes to unhealthy coping behaviors, excessive alcohol use, poor dietary choices, sedentary lifestyles, insufficient sleep. Workplace happiness supports healthy behaviors, regular exercise, better nutrition, adequate sleep, moderate substance use.

Public health costs of workplace-induced health problems run into trillions globally. The $8.8 trillion global cost of disengagement documented in Chapter 7 from Gallup (2023) includes but isn't limited to health costs. Separate accounting of healthcare costs attributable to workplace stress suggests over $1 trillion annually in the United States alone could be saved through improved workplace conditions.

The implications for healthcare systems are profound. Healthcare costs continue escalating despite medical advances partly because we're treating symptoms of social determinants of health, including workplace conditions, rather than addressing root causes. Improving workplace conditions could do more to reduce healthcare costs than many medical interventions because it addresses upstream factors that prevent health problems rather than treating problems after they develop.

Economic Innovation and Productivity

At societal level, the aggregate effects of workplace engagement affect economic performance and innovation capacity. Research at the organizational level shows clear patterns: companies with higher employee engagement demonstrate higher innovation rates, stronger financial performance, better productivity, and generally superior business outcomes (Harter et al., 2020). While extending these findings to national economies requires caution, the logic suggests that countries fostering widespread workplace satisfaction would benefit from similar advantages at scale.

The relationship operates through multiple mechanisms. Happy, engaged workforces innovate more consistently, generating new products, processes, and solutions that drive economic advancement. They work more productively, creating more value per hour worked. They stick with employers longer, reducing the economic costs of turnover and preserving institutional knowledge.

The policy implications are significant. Economic development strategies focusing solely on infrastructure, education, or business incentives miss the importance of workplace quality. Regions that prioritize workplace satisfaction alongside traditional economic development priorities may achieve better long-term economic outcomes.

The Virtuous Cycle: Reinforcing Positive Effects

The ripple effects of workplace happiness don't just radiate outward, they create feedback loops that reinforce and amplify effects. Happy employees create engaged families, which produce healthier children, who become more capable adults, who build stronger communities, which create better conditions for business, which enables better workplaces.

This virtuous cycle can be envisioned operating at multiple levels:

Individual level: Workplace happiness improves health and relationships, which supports better work performance, which creates more workplace success and satisfaction.

Organizational level: Employee engagement drives better business results, which creates resources for further investment in employees, which builds more engagement.

Community level: Workplace satisfaction enables civic engagement, which strengthens communities, which become more attractive locations for business and talent, which supports better employment.

Societal level: Aggregate workplace happiness improves public health and economic performance, which creates prosperity supporting better workplace conditions, which generates more happiness.

The converse is also true evidenced in vicious cycles where workplace misery cascades into family stress, community deterioration, public health problems, and economic struggles that make workplace improvement more difficult. Breaking these negative cycles requires intervention, but once broken, virtuous cycles can develop.

Improvements in workplace satisfaction can correlate with improvements in community indicators, which correlate with improved business performance, which enables further workplace investment. The cycles accelerate over time as effects compound.

The Measurement Challenge: Documenting Ripple Effects

Quantifying ripple effects presents methodological challenges. The effects are real but distributed across multiple domains, family wellbeing, community vitality, public health, economic performance. Isolating workplace happiness as a causal factor requires controlling for numerous confounding variables. Tracking longitudinal data that changes over time is expensive and complex.

The accumulating evidence from diverse methods and contexts increasingly supports the reality of substantial ripple effects. Workplace happiness matters not just for organizational outcomes but for family wellbeing, community vitality, public health, economic prosperity, and democratic stability. The effects are real, measurable, and substantial.

The Imperative: Workplace Happiness as Social Responsibility

Understanding ripple effects reframes workplace happiness from optional nicety to social imperative. When we recognize that workplace conditions affect not just employees but their families, their communities, and society broadly, the ethical calculation changes and puts much greater pressure on managers and leaders to do the right thing in creating happy employees.

Organizations don't exist in isolation, they're embedded in communities and societies. The conditions they create inside their walls radiate outward, affecting people who never chose to be affected. When workplaces systematically make people miserable, the collateral damage extends across families and communities. When workplaces create genuine happiness, the benefits flow broadly as well.

This reality creates moral responsibilities beyond shareholder returns. Organizations have obligations not just to shareholders but to employees, their families, their communities, and society broadly. Creating workplace happiness isn't just good business, it's good citizenship.

The evidence demonstrates that these moral and business imperatives align. Organizations that create genuine workplace happiness achieve better business results (Harter et al., 2020) while also contributing to employee wellbeing that extends beyond work into families and communities (Ten Brummelhuis & Bakker, 2012). Doing well and doing good are not opposing objectives but reinforcing strategies. The old dichotomy between doing well and doing good dissolves, they're mutually reinforcing when approached thoughtfully.

Conclusion: The Ripples We Choose to Create

Every organization creates ripples, the question is whether those ripples lift or drag down everything they touch. Workplaces that systematically create misery send exhausted, depleted people into families and communities, reducing human flourishing at every level. Workplaces that create genuine happiness energize families, strengthen communities, improve public health, and support democratic culture.

We stand at a moment of unusual clarity about these dynamics. Decades of research document the ripple effects. We know workplace conditions matter far beyond organizational boundaries. We know the costs of getting it wrong and the benefits of getting it right. We know what practices create happiness and what practices destroy it.

The question isn't whether workplace happiness creates beneficial ripple effects, the research clearly demonstrates it does. The question is whether organizations will take responsibility for the ripples they create, whether they'll invest in creating positive rather than negative effects, whether they'll recognize that workplace happiness is a social contribution as much as a business strategy.

The opportunity is profound. Organizations collectively employing hundreds of millions of people could, through improved workplace practices, strengthen families, build communities, improve public health, boost economic performance, and support democratic stability. The investment required is modest compared to these potential returns. The practices are well-documented. The barriers are real but are possible to overcome.

What's required is choice, the choice to create ripples of happiness rather than misery, to invest in human flourishing rather than accepting human suffering, to recognize that how we organize work shapes not just organizational outcomes but human civilization.

The ripples are real. The choice is yours. What will you create? How will the memory of your words and actions to the people under your care and responsibility be carried into the future by the generations of families you affected in the work place?

About the Author

Education
- Ph.D. in Organization and Management, Capella University
- M.S. in Marketing: Digital Marketing, Southern New Hampshire University
- M.A. in Executive Leadership, Liberty University
- M.A. in Strategic Communication, Liberty University
- M.B.A., Fontbonne College
- B.S., Fontbonne College
- Graduate Certificate in Management and Leadership, Liberty University

Chris Huseman, Ph.D., is a dynamic speaker, award-winning business professor, entrepreneur and trusted advisor to Fortune 500 companies and more. With more than 30 years of experience at the intersection of leadership, strategy, and performance, Chris has become a sought-after voice for organizations looking to spark transformation. His work spans industries and continents, with clients ranging from global enterprises to entrepreneurial teams eager to elevate their game.

Chris brings more than just theory, he brings the grit. As a past Ironman triathlete, Chris lives the discipline and perseverance he teaches. Whether guiding executives through high-stakes decisions or inspiring audiences from the stage, his message is grounded in action, endurance, and results. His persistent mindset is reflected in every talk: train hard, lead well, and finish strong. In addition to his corporate impact, Chris has been recognized as an award-winning professor of business, known for his engaging style and deep expertise in marketing, sales, and digital strategy. For more than 20 years, his classes are often described as transformational, as he has mentored countless students into successful careers. His academic credibility reinforces the practical tools he delivers in every keynote or training session.

A proud father of six, Chris weaves authenticity and relatability into everything he does. Audiences connect with his straightforward, real-world approach, no fluff, just fresh insights and tested tactics that people can actually use. He believes in helping leaders and teams cut through complexity, find clarity, and take action immediately.

Chris's presentations are packed with usable frameworks, high-impact stories, and the kind of strategic thinking that sticks. He has received numerous accolades from clients, students, and colleagues alike for his ability to unlock potential, ignite enthusiasm, and drive measurable progress. Whether on stage or in a boardroom, he challenges people to think differently, and gives them the tools to do it.

If you're looking for a speaker who combines academic depth with real-world experience, Dr. Huseman is for you. He doesn't just speak to crowds, he connects, equips, and inspires them to lead with purpose, resilience, and results.

You can contact Dr. Huseman by visiting:
http://www.husemanleadership.com.

Notes

Introduction

5 Gallup. (2022). State of the global workplace: 2022 report. Gallup Press

7 Gallup. (2023). The world's $8.8 trillion workplace problem. https://www.gallup.com/workplace/393497/world-trillion-workplace-problem.aspx.

Chapter 1 The 43 Million: When One-Third of Workers Lose Their Drive

15 Robinson, C. (2025). From drift to drive: A high achiever's guide to breaking the chains of complacency. Maxwell Leadership. Page 23

16 Harter, J. K., Schmidt, F. L., Agrawal, S., Plowman, S. K., & Blue, A. (2020). The relationship between engagement at work and organizational outcomes: 2020 Q12 meta-analysis (10th ed.). Gallup.

16 Steelman, L. A., Levy, P. E., & Snell, A. F. (2004). The feedback environment scale: Construct definition, measurement, and validation. Educational and Psychological Measurement, 64(1), 165-184.

16 Morrison, E. W. (2014). Employee voice and silence. Annual Review of Organizational Psychology and Organizational Behavior, 1, 173-197.

16 Maslach, C., & Leiter, M. P. (2008). Early predictors of job burnout and engagement. Journal of Applied Psychology, 93(3), 498-512.

20 Gallup. (2015). State of the American manager: Analytics and advice for leaders. Gallup Press.

20 Skogstad, A., Einarsen, S., Torsheim, T., Aasland, M. S., & Hetland, H. (2007). The destructiveness of laissez-faire leadership behavior. Journal of Occupational Health Psychology, 12(1), 80-92.

20 Tepper, B. J. (2000). Consequences of abusive supervision. Academy of Management Journal, 43(2), 178-190.

23 Men, L. R. (2014). Why leadership matters to internal communication: Linking transformational leadership, symmetrical communication, and employee outcomes. Journal of Public Relations Research, 26(3), 256-279. https://doi.org/10.1080/1062726X.2014.908719

23 Colquitt, J. A., Conlon, D. E., Wesson, M. J., Porter, C. O. L. H., & Ng, K. Y. (2001). Justice at the millennium: A meta-analytic review of 25 years of organizational justice research. Journal of Applied Psychology, 86(3), 425-445. https://doi.org/10.1037/0021-9010.86.3.425

24 Edmondson, A. C. (1999). Psychological safety and learning behavior in work teams. Administrative Science Quarterly, 44(2), 350-383. https://doi.org/10.2307/2666999

24 Shuck, B., Twyford, D., Reio, T. G., & Shuck, A. (2014). Human resource development practices and employee engagement: Examining the connection with employee turnover intentions. Human Resource Development Quarterly, 25(2), 239-270. https://doi.org/10.1002/hrdq.21190

24 Deal, J. J., Stawiski, S., Graves, L., Gentry, W. A., Weber, T. J., & Ruderman, M. (2013). Motivation at work: Which matters more, generation or managerial level? Consulting Psychology Journal: Practice and Research, 65(1), 1-16. https://doi.org/10.1037/a0032693

25 Ng, T. W. H., & Feldman, D. C. (2015). The moderating effects of age in the relationships of job autonomy to work outcomes. Work, Aging and Retirement, 1(1), 64-78. https://doi.org/10.1093/workar/wau003

25 Allen, D. G., Bryant, P. C., & Vardaman, J. M. (2010). Retaining talent: Replacing misconceptions with evidence-based strategies. Academy of Management Perspectives, 24(2), 48-64. https://doi.org/10.5465/amp.24.2.48

25 Bailey, C., Madden, A., Alfes, K., & Fletcher, L. (2017). The meaning, antecedents and outcomes of employee engagement: A

narrative synthesis. International Journal of Management Reviews, 19(1), 31-53. https://doi.org/10.1111/ijmr.12077

25 Shuck, B., Twyford, D., Reio, T. G., & Shuck, A. (2014). Human resource development practices and employee engagement: Examining the connection with employee turnover intentions. Human Resource Development Quarterly, 25(2), 239-270. https://doi.org/10.1002/hrdq.21190

25 Bakker, A. B., Demerouti, E., & Sanz-Vergel, A. I. (2014). Burnout and work engagement: The JD-R approach. Annual Review of Organizational Psychology and Organizational Behavior, 1(1), 389-411. https://doi.org/10.1146/annurev-orgpsych-031413-091235

26 Kim, E., & Glomb, T. M. (2014). Victimization of high performers: The roles of envy and work group identification. Journal of Applied Psychology, 99(4), 619-634. https://doi.org/10.1037/a0035789

26 Solinger, O. N., van Olffen, W., Roe, R. A., & Hofmans, J. (2013). On becoming (un)committed: A taxonomy and test of newcomer onboarding scenarios. Organization Science, 24(6), 1640-1661. https://doi.org/10.1287/orsc.1120.0818

26 Bakker, A. B., Demerouti, E., & Sanz-Vergel, A. I. (2014). Burnout and work engagement: The JD-R approach. Annual Review of Organizational Psychology and Organizational Behavior, 1(1), 389-411. https://doi.org/10.1146/annurev-orgpsych-031413-091235

26 Barsade, S. G., & Gibson, D. E. (2012). Group affect: Its influence on individual and group outcomes. Current Directions in Psychological Science, 21(2), 119-123. https://doi.org/10.1177/0963721412438352

28 Vaden, R. (2012). Take the stairs: 7 steps to achieving true success. TarcherPerigee. Page175

28 Allen, J. (2020). Get out of your head: Stopping the spiral of toxic thoughts. WaterBrook Press. Page 43

Chapter 2 The Happiness Advantage: Building Profitable Organizations Through Well-Being

32 Achor, S. (2010). The happiness advantage: The seven principles of positive psychology that fuel success and performance at work. Crown Business.

32 Fredrickson, B. L., & Branigan, C. (2005). Positive emotions broaden the scope of attention and thought-action repertoires. Cognition & Emotion, 19(3), 313-332. https://doi.org/10.1080/02699930441000238

33 Bakker, A. B., & Demerouti, E. (2017). Job demands-resources theory: Taking stock and looking forward. Journal of Occupational Health Psychology, 22(3), 273-285. https://doi.org/10.1037/ocp0000056

33 Kok, B. E., Coffey, K. A., Cohn, M. A., Catalino, L. I., Vacharkulksemsuk, T., Algoe, S. B., Brantley, M., & Fredrickson, B. L. (2013). How positive emotions build physical health: Perceived positive social connections account for the upward spiral between positive emotions and vagal tone. Psychological Science, 24(7), 1123-1132. https://doi.org/10.1177/0956797612470827

33 Diener, E., & Seligman, M. E. P. (2004). Beyond money: Toward an economy of well-being. Psychological Science in the Public Interest, 5(1), 1-31. https://doi.org/10.1111/j.0963-7214.2004.00501001.x

34 Oswald, A. J., Proto, E., & Sgroi, D. (2015). Happiness and productivity. Journal of Labor Economics, 33(4), 789-822. https://doi.org/10.1086/681096

34 Rich, B. L., Lepine, J. A., & Crawford, E. R. (2010). Job engagement: Antecedents and effects on job performance. Academy of Management Journal, 53(3), 617-635. https://doi.org/10.5465/amj.2010.51468988

35 Davis, M. A. (2009). Understanding the relationship between mood and creativity: A meta-analysis. Organizational Behavior and Human Decision Processes, 108(1), 25-38. https://doi.org/10.1016/j.obhdp.2008.04.001

35 Gloria, C. T., & Steinhardt, M. A. (2016). Relationships among positive emotions, coping, resilience and mental health. Stress and Health, 32(2), 145-156. https://doi.org/10.1002/smi.2589

37 Edmondson, A. C. (1999). Psychological safety and learning behavior in work teams. Administrative Science Quarterly, 44(2), 350-383. https://doi.org/10.2307/2666999

37 Fowler, J. H., & Christakis, N. A. (2008). Dynamic spread of happiness in a large social network: Longitudinal analysis over 20 years in the Framingham Heart Study. BMJ, 337, a2338. https://doi.org/10.1136/bmj.a2338

38 Edmondson, A. C. (1999). Psychological safety and learning behavior in work teams. Administrative Science Quarterly, 44(2), 350-383. https://doi.org/10.2307/2666999

38 Wang, S., & Noe, R. A. (2010). Knowledge sharing: A review and directions for future research. Human Resource Management Review, 20(2), 115-131. https://doi.org/10.1016/j.hrmr.2009.10.001

39 Gallup. (2022). State of the global workplace: 2022 report. Gallup Press.

40 Edmans, A. (2011). Does the stock market fully value intangibles? Employee satisfaction and equity prices. Journal of Financial Economics, 101(3), 621-640. https://doi.org/10.1016/j.jfineco.2011.03.021

40 Edmans, A. (2012). The link between job satisfaction and firm value, with implications for corporate social responsibility. Academy of Management Perspectives, 26(4), 1-19. https://doi.org/10.5465/amp.2012.0046

40 Harter, J. K., Schmidt, F. L., & Hayes, T. L. (2002). Business-unit-level relationship between employee satisfaction, employee engagement, and business outcomes: A meta-analysis. Journal of Applied Psychology, 87(2), 268-279. https://doi.org/10.1037/0021-9010.87.2.268

41 Laschinger, H. K. S., & Leiter, M. P. (2006). The impact of nursing work environments on patient safety outcomes: The mediating role of burnout/engagement. Journal of Nursing Administration, 36(5), 259-267. https://doi.org/10.1097/00005110-200605000-00019

41 Harter, J. K., Schmidt, F. L., Agrawal, S., Plowman, S. K., & Blue, A. (2020). The relationship between engagement at work and organizational outcomes: 2020 Q12 meta-analysis: 10th edition. Gallup.

41 Knight, C., Patterson, M., & Dawson, J. (2017). Building work engagement: A systematic review and meta-analysis investigating the effectiveness of work engagement interventions. Journal of Organizational Behavior, 38(6), 792-812. https://doi.org/10.1002/job.2167

42 Schneider, B., Macey, W. H., Barbera, K. M., & Martin, N. (2009). Driving customer satisfaction and financial success through employee engagement. People and Strategy, 32(2), 22-27.

42 Allen, D. G., Bryant, P. C., & Vardaman, J. M. (2010). Retaining talent: Replacing misconceptions with evidence-based strategies. Academy of Management Perspectives, 24(2), 48-64. https://doi.org/10.5465/amp.24.2.48

42 Wright, P. M., Dunford, B. B., & Snell, S. A. (2001). Human resources and the resource based view of the firm. Journal of Management, 27(6), 701-721. https://doi.org/10.1177/014920630102700607

43 Achor, S. (2010). The happiness advantage: The seven principles of positive psychology that fuel success and performance at work. Crown Business.

44 Achor, S. (2010). The happiness advantage: The seven principles of positive psychology that fuel success and performance at work. Crown Business.

46 Achor, S. (2010). The happiness advantage: The seven principles of positive psychology that fuel success and performance at work. Crown Business.

Chapter 3 The 13% Advantage: Do employees need to be happy at work to be productive?

49 Grant, A. M. (2016). Originals: How non-conformists move the world. Viking/Penguin Random House. Page 14

49 Kotter, J. P. (2012). Leading change. Harvard Business Review Press. Pages 116 and 119

49 Sinek, S. (2014). Leaders eat last: Why some teams pull together and others don't. Portfolio/Penguin. Page 169

49 Ramsey, D. (2011). EntreLeadership: 20 years of practical business wisdom from the trenches. Howard Books. Page 228

49 Friedman, R. (2014). The best place to work: The art and science of creating an extraordinary workplace. Perigee Book. Page 94

50 Edmondson, A. C. (1999). Psychological safety and learning behavior in work teams. Administrative Science Quarterly, 44(2), 350-383. https://doi.org/10.2307/2666999

51 Edmondson, A. C., & Lei, Z. (2014). Psychological safety: The history, renaissance, and future of an interpersonal construct. Annual Review of Organizational Psychology and Organizational Behavior, 1(1), 23-43. https://doi.org/10.1146/annurev-orgpsych-031413-091305

51-53 Gallup. (2022). State of the global workplace: 2022 report. Gallup Press.

53 MIT Sloan School of Management. (2023). Health and happiness as drivers of employment decisions. MIT Research Report.

54 Judge, T. A., Piccolo, R. F., Podsakoff, N. P., Shaw, J. C., & Rich, B. L. (2010). The relationship between pay and job satisfaction: A meta-analysis of the literature. Journal of Vocational Behavior, 77(2), 157-167

54 Kahneman, D., & Deaton, A. (2010). High income improves evaluation of life but not emotional well-being. Proceedings of the National Academy of Sciences, 107(38), 16489-16493.

54 Burbano, V. C. (2016). Social responsibility messages and worker wage requirements: Field experimental evidence from online labor marketplaces. Organization Science, 27(4), 1010-1028.

54 Griffeth, R. W., Hom, P. W., & Gaertner, S. (2000). A meta-analysis of antecedents and correlates of employee turnover: Update, moderator tests, and research implications for the next millennium. Journal of Management, 26(3), 463-488.

55 University of Oxford, Saïd Business School. (2023). Social happiness and productivity: Evidence from a large-scale field experiment. Journal of Labor Economics, 41(3), 819-859.

56 Pew Research Center. (2021). Where Americans find meaning in life. Pew Research Center Report.

60 Edmondson, A. C. (1999). Psychological safety and learning behavior in work teams. Administrative Science Quarterly, 44(2), 350-383. https://doi.org/10.2307/2666999

Chapter 4 If employee happiness contributes to productivity, shouldn't companies strive to make their employees happy?

64 Smith, A. (1776/2003). The wealth of nations. Bantam Classics. (Original work published 1776)

65 Friedman, M. (1970). The social responsibility of business is to increase its profits. The New York Times Magazine.

68 Guidara, W. (2022). Unreasonable hospitality: The remarkable power of giving people more than they expect. Optimism Press.

69 Robinson, C. (2025). From drift to drive: A high achiever's guide to breaking the chains of complacency. Maxwell Leadership.

69 Lewis, T. W. (2020). Solid ground: A foundation for winning in work and in life. T.W. Lewis Company.

72 Bakker, A. B., & Demerouti, E. (2008). Towards a model of work engagement. Career Development International, 13(3), 209-223.

73 Gallup. (2022). State of the global workplace: 2022 report. Gallup Press.

74 Gallup, Inc. (2020). State of the global workplace: 2020 report. Gallup Press. https://www.gallup.com/workplace/

74 Fortune Media IP Limited. (2019). 100 best companies to work for. https://fortune.com/best-companies/

74 Edmans, A. (2011). Does the stock market fully value intangibles? Employee satisfaction and equity prices. Journal of Financial Economics, 101(3), 621–640. https://doi.org/10.1016/j.jfineco.2011.03.021

75 Gallup, Inc. (2020). State of the global workplace: 2020 report. Gallup Press. https://www.gallup.com/workplace/

75 De Neve, J.-E., Oswald, A. J., Krekel, C., & Ward, G. (2023). Employee well-being, productivity, and firm performance. Management Science, 69(5), 2521–2543. https://doi.org/10.1287/mnsc.2022.4501

75 Cameron, K. S. (2012). Positive leadership: Strategies for extraordinary performance. Berrett-Koehler.

76 Freeman, R. E. (1984). Strategic management: A stakeholder approach. Pitman.

77 Business Roundtable. (2019, August 19). Business Roundtable redefines the purpose of a corporation to promote "an economy that serves all Americans" [Press release]. Business Roundtable. https://www.businessroundtable.org/business-roundtable-redefines-the-

purpose-of-a-corporation-to-promote-an-economy-that-serves-all-americans

Chapter 5 The Responsibility Matrix: Who Owns Employee Happiness in the Modern Workplace?

87 Zhuo, J., & Stanley, P. (2019). The making of a manager: What to do when everyone looks to you. Portfolio/Penguin. Page 33

87 Scroggins, C. (2017). How to lead when you're not in charge: Leveraging influence when you lack authority. Zondervan. Page 95

87 Maxwell, J. C. (2011). The 5 levels of leadership: Proven steps to maximize your potential. Center Street. Page 257

90 Graen, G. B., & Uhl-Bien, M. (1995). Relationship-based approach to leadership: Development of leader–member exchange (LMX) theory of leadership over 25 years: Applying a multi-level multi-domain perspective. Leadership Quarterly, 6(2), 219–247. https://doi.org/10.1016/1048-9843(95)90036-5

90 Uhl-Bien, M. (2012). Relational leadership theory: Exploring the social processes of leadership and organizing. Leadership Quarterly, 23(6), 654–676. https://doi.org/10.1016/j.leaqua.2012.10.007

91 Edmondson, A. C. (1999). Psychological safety and learning behavior in work teams. Administrative Science Quarterly, 44(2), 350-383.

91 Achor, S. (2010). The happiness advantage: The seven principles of positive psychology that fuel success and performance at work. Crown Business.

92 Gallup. (2022). State of the global workplace: 2022 report. Gallup Press.

95 Judge, T. A., Heller, D., & Mount, M. K. (2002). Five-factor model of personality and job satisfaction: A meta-analysis. Journal of Applied

Psychology, 87(3), 530–541. https://doi.org/10.1037/0021-9010.87.3.530

95 Lyubomirsky, S., Sheldon, K. M., & Schkade, D. (2005). Pursuing happiness: The architecture of sustainable change. Review of General Psychology, 9(2), 111–131. https://doi.org/10.1037/1089-2680.9.2.111

95 Gallup, Inc. (2020). State of the global workplace: 2020 report. Gallup Press. https://www.gallup.com/workplace/

97 EtherWorld.com. (2024). Manager responsibility for employee happiness: Global workplace study.

100 Dollard, M. F., & Bakker, A. B. (2010). Psychosocial safety climate as a precursor to conducive work environments, psychological health problems, and employee engagement. Journal of Occupational and Organizational Psychology, 83(3), 579-599.

100 Dollard, M. F., & Bakker, A. B. (2010). Psychosocial safety climate as a precursor to conducive work environments, psychological health problems, and employee engagement. Journal of Occupational and Organizational Psychology, 83(3), 579-599.

100 Law, R., Dollard, M. F., Tuckey, M. R., & Dormann, C. (2011). Psychosocial safety climate as a lead indicator of workplace bullying and harassment, job resources, psychological health and employee engagement. Accident Analysis & Prevention, 43(5), 1782-1793.

100 Zadow, A. J., Dollard, M. F., Mclinton, S. S., Lawrence, P., & Tuckey, M. R. (2017). Psychosocial safety climate, emotional exhaustion, and work injuries in healthcare workplaces. Stress and Health, 33(5), 558-569.

101 Edmondson, A. C. (1999). Psychological safety and learning behavior in work teams. Administrative Science Quarterly, 44(2), 350-383.

Chapter 6 The Manager's Toolkit: Evidence-Based Strategies for Fostering Employee Happiness

104 Barsade, S. G., & Gibson, D. E. (2012). Group affect: Its influence on individual and group outcomes. Current Directions in Psychological Science, 21(2), 119-123. https://doi.org/10.1177/0963721412438352

105 Edmondson, A. C. (1999). Psychological safety and learning behavior in work teams. Administrative Science Quarterly, 44(2), 350-383.

104 Rizzolatti, G., & Craighero, L. (2004). The mirror-neuron system. Annual Review of Neuroscience, 27, 169-192.

104 Bastiaansen, J. A., Thioux, M., & Keysers, C. (2009). Evidence for mirror systems in emotions. Philosophical Transactions of the Royal Society B: Biological Sciences, 364(1528), 2391-2404.

104 Hatfield, E., Cacioppo, J. T., & Rapson, R. L. (1994). Emotional contagion. Cambridge University Press.

104 Sy, T., Côté, S., & Saavedra, R. (2005). The contagious leader: Impact of the leader's mood on the mood of group members, group affective tone, and group processes. Journal of Applied Psychology, 90(2), 295-305.

104 Hoobler, J. M., & Brass, D. J. (2006). Abusive supervision and family undermining as displaced aggression. Journal of Applied Psychology, 91(5), 1125-1133.

108 Harter, J. K., Schmidt, F. L., & Hayes, T. L. (2002). Business-unit-level relationship between employee satisfaction, employee engagement, and business outcomes: A meta-analysis. Journal of Applied Psychology, 87(2), 268-279. https://doi.org/10.1037/0021-9010.87.2.268

109 Brotman, A., & Sack, A. (2025). AI First: The playbook for a future-proof business and brand. Harvard Business Review Press.

110 Duhigg, C. (2024). Supercommunicators: How to unlock the secret language of connection. Random House.

111 Men, L. R. (2014). Why leadership matters to internal communication: Linking transformational leadership, symmetrical communication, and employee outcomes. Journal of Public Relations Research, 26(3), 256-279. https://doi.org/10.1080/1062726X.2014.908719

111 Johlke, M. C., & Duhan, D. F. (2000). Supervisor communication practices and service employee job outcomes. Journal of Service Research, 3(2), 154-165. https://doi.org/10.1177/109467050032004

112 Bordia, P., Hunt, E., Paulsen, N., Tourish, D., & DiFonzo, N. (2004). Uncertainty during organizational change: Is it all about control? European Journal of Work and Organizational Psychology, 13(3), 345-365. https://doi.org/10.1080/13594320444000128

113 Rosso, B. D., Dekas, K. H., & Wrzesniewski, A. (2010). On the meaning of work: A theoretical integration and review. Research in Organizational Behavior, 30, 91-127. https://doi.org/10.1016/j.riob.2010.09.001

113 Steger, M. F., Dik, B. J., & Duffy, R. D. (2012). Measuring meaningful work: The Work and Meaning Inventory (WAMI). Journal of Career Assessment, 20(3), 322-337. https://doi.org/10.1177/1069072711436160

114 Dweck, C. S. (2006). Mindset: The new psychology of success. Random House.

114 Caniëls, M. C. J., Semeijn, J. H., & Renders, I. H. M. (2018). Mind the mindset! The interaction of proactive personality, transformational leadership and growth mindset for engagement at work. Career Development International, 23(1), 48-66. https://doi.org/10.1108/CDI-11-2016-0194

115 Buffini & Company. (2024, October 3). Follow-up , The key to trust in business and relationships. Buffini & Company Blog. https://blog.buffini.com/follow-up-the-key-to-trust-in-business-and-relationships-buffini/

116 Zhuo, J., & Stanley, P. (2019). The making of a manager: What to do when everyone looks to you. Portfolio/Penguin. Page 36 and 61

116 Holtz, L. (2007). Wins, losses, and lessons: An autobiography. HarperEntertainment. Page 207

116 Covey, S. M. R., Kasperson, D., Covey, M., & Judd, G. T. (2022). Trust & inspire: How truly great leaders unleash greatness in others. Simon & Schuster. Page 45

117 Schnackenberg, A. K., & Tomlinson, E. C. (2016). Organizational transparency: A new perspective on managing trust in organization-stakeholder relationships. Journal of Management, 42(7), 1784-1810. https://doi.org/10.1177/0149206314525202

117 Men, L. R., & Stacks, D. (2014). The effects of authentic leadership on strategic internal communication and employee-organization relationships. Journal of Public Relations Research, 26(4), 301-324. https://doi.org/10.1080/1062726X.2014.908720

117 Rawlins, B. (2008). Measuring the relationship between organizational transparency and employee trust. Public Relations Journal, 2(2), 1-21.

118 Breevaart, K., Bakker, A., Hetland, J., Demerouti, E., Olsen, O. K., & Espevik, R. (2014). Daily transactional and transformational leadership and daily employee engagement. Journal of Occupational and Organizational Psychology, 87(1), 138-157. https://doi.org/10.1111/joop.12041

118 Wang, G., Oh, I. S., Courtright, S. H., & Colbert, A. E. (2011). Transformational leadership and performance across criteria and levels: A meta-analytic review of 25 years of research. Group & Organization Management, 36(2), 223-270. https://doi.org/10.1177/1059601111401017

119-120 Locke, E. A., & Latham, G. P. (2002). Building a practically useful theory of goal setting and task motivation: A 35-year odyssey. American Psychologist, 57(9), 705-717.

120 Barsade, S. G., & Gibson, D. E. (2012). Group affect: Its influence on individual and group outcomes. Current Directions in Psychological Science, 21(2), 119-123. https://doi.org/10.1177/0963721412438352

120 Chi, N. W., Chung, Y. Y., & Tsai, W. C. (2011). How do happy leaders enhance team success? The mediating roles of transformational leadership, group affective tone, and team processes. Journal of Applied Social Psychology, 41(6), 1421-1454. https://doi.org/10.1111/j.1559-1816.2011.00767.x

121 Seligman, M. E. P. (1990). Learned optimism: How to change your mind and your life. Knopf.

121   Amabile, T., & Kramer, S. (2011). The progress principle: Using small wins to ignite joy, engagement, and creativity at work. Harvard Business Review Press.

122 Heslin, P. A., Vandewalle, D., & Latham, G. P. (2006). Keen to help? Managers' implicit person theories and their subsequent employee coaching. Personnel Psychology, 59(4), 871-902. https://doi.org/10.1111/j.1744-6570.2006.00057.x

122 Tulgan, B. (2017). The 27 challenges managers face: Step-by-step solutions to (nearly) all of your management problems. RainmakerThinking.

122 Tulgan, B. (2024, July 19). The basics of good one-on-one meetings. Forbes. https://www.forbes.com/sites/brucetulgan/2024/07/19/the-basics-of-good-one-on-one-meetings/

123 Baumeister, R. F., & Leary, M. R. (1995). The need to belong: Desire for interpersonal attachments as a fundamental human motivation. Psychological Bulletin, 117(3), 497-529. https://doi.org/10.1037/0033-2909.117.3.497

123 Van den Broeck, A., Ferris, D. L., Chang, C. H., & Rosen, C. C. (2016). A review of self-determination theory's basic psychological

needs at work. Journal of Management, 42(5), 1195-1229.
https://doi.org/10.1177/0149206316632058

123 Cockshaw, W. D., Shochet, I. M., & Obst, P. L. (2013). General belongingness, workplace belongingness, and depressive symptoms. Journal of Community & Applied Social Psychology, 23(3), 240-251. https://doi.org/10.1002/casp.2121

124 Van den Broeck, A., Ferris, D. L., Chang, C. H., & Rosen, C. C. (2016). A review of self-determination theory's basic psychological needs at work. Journal of Management, 42(5), 1195-1229. https://doi.org/10.1177/0149206316632058

125 Avolio, B. J., & Gardner, W. L. (2005). Authentic leadership development: Getting to the root of positive forms of leadership. The Leadership Quarterly, 16(3), 315-338. https://doi.org/10.1016/j.leaqua.2005.03.001

Chapter 7 The Hidden Crisis: How Employee Disengagement Drains Global Profitability

129 Gallup. (2022). State of the global workplace: 2022 report. Gallup Press.

130 Gallup. (2022). State of the global workplace: 2022 report. Gallup Press.

131 Boushey, H., & Glynn, S. J. (2012). There are significant business costs to replacing employees. Center for American Progress. https://www.americanprogress.org/article/there-are-significant-business-costs-to-replacing-employees/

132 Dyerly, R. (2025, January 21). The myth of replaceability: Preparing for the loss of key employees. SHRM Executive Network. https://www.shrm.org/executive-network/insights/myth-replaceability-preparing-loss-key-employees/

132 Felps, W., Mitchell, T. R., Hekman, D. R., Lee, T. W., Holtom, B. C., & Harman, W. S. (2009). Turnover contagion: How coworkers' job

embeddedness and job search behaviors influence quitting. Academy of Management Journal, 52(3), 545-561. https://doi.org/10.5465/amj.2009.41331075

133 ActivTrak. (2024, July 4). Exploring the true cost of disengaged employees. ActivTrak. https://www.activtrak.com/blog/cost-of-disengaged-employees

133 Kaiser Permanente. (2022). The impact of disengagement on absenteeism and healthcare costs. Kaiser Permanente Research Institute.

133 Schaufeli, W. B., Bakker, A. B., & Van Rhenen, W. (2009). How changes in job demands and resources predict burnout, work engagement, and sickness absenteeism. Journal of Organizational Behavior, 30(7), 893-917. https://doi.org/10.1002/job.595

134 Kuoppala, J., Lamminpää, A., Liira, J., & Vainio, H. (2008). Leadership, job well-being, and health effects, A systematic review and a meta-analysis. Journal of Occupational and Environmental Medicine, 50(8), 904-915. https://doi.org/10.1097/JOM.0b013e31817e918d

134 American Institute of Stress. (2024, July 5). 80% of employees report 'productivity anxiety' and lower well-being in new study. Stress.org. https://www.stress.org/news/80-of-employees-report-productivity-anxiety-and-lower-well-being-in-new-study/

135 American Institute of Stress. (2022, April 20). What is the true cost of work-related stress? Stress.org. https://www.stress.org/news/what-is-the-true-cost-of-work-related-stress/

135 Gallup. (2022). State of the global workplace: 2022 report. Gallup Press.

136 Occupational Safety and Health Administration. (n.d.). Long-term stress harms everyone in the workplace (Workplace Stress Toolkit). U.S. Department of Labor. https://www.osha.gov/sites/default/files/Long-Term_Stress_Harms_Workplace_Stress_Toolkit_revised_508.pdf

136 Clifford, C. (2015, May 10). Unhappy workers cost the U.S. up to $550 billion a year (infographic). Entrepreneur. https://www.entrepreneur.com/leadership/unhappy-workers-cost-the-us-up-to-550-billion-a-year/246036

136 Gallup. (2022). State of the global workplace: 2022 report. Gallup Press.

137 Detert, J. R., & Burris, E. R. (2007). Leadership behavior and employee voice: Is the door really open? Academy of Management Journal, 50(4), 869-884. https://doi.org/10.5465/amj.2007.26279183

137 Solinger, O. N., van Olffen, W., Roe, R. A., & Hofmans, J. (2013). On becoming (un)committed: A taxonomy and test of newcomer onboarding scenarios. Organization Science, 24(6), 1640-1661. https://doi.org/10.1287/orsc.1120.0818

138 Gallup, Inc. (2023). How to improve employee engagement in the workplace. Gallup. https://www.gallup.com/workplace/285674/improve-employee-engagement-workplace.aspx

139 Kumar, V., & Reinartz, W. (2016). Creating enduring customer value. Journal of Marketing, 80(6), 36-68. https://doi.org/10.1509/jm.15.0414

140 Gallup. (2022). State of the global workplace: 2022 report. Gallup Press.

141 Diener, E., & Seligman, M. E. P. (2004). Beyond money: Toward an economy of well-being. Psychological Science in the Public Interest, 5(1), 1-31. https://doi.org/10.1111/j.0963-7214.2004.00501001.x

Chapter 8 The Biblical Mandate of Encouragement in Leadership and Employee Happiness

146 Luthans, F., Youssef, C. M., & Avolio, B. J. (2007). Psychological capital: Developing the human competitive edge. Oxford University Press.

147-148 Edmondson, A. C. (1999). Psychological safety and learning behavior in work teams. Administrative Science Quarterly, 44(2), 350-383.

148 Steelman, L. A., Levy, P. E., & Snell, A. F. (2004). The feedback environment scale: Construct definition, measurement, and validation. Educational and Psychological Measurement, 64(1), 165-184. https://doi.org/10.1177/0013164403258440

150 Gottman, J. M. (1994). What predicts divorce? The relationship between marital processes and marital outcomes. Lawrence Erlbaum Associates.

151 Daniels, A. C. (1994). Bringing out the best in people: How to apply the astonishing power of positive reinforcement. McGraw-Hill.

153 Hersey, P., & Blanchard, K. H. (1969). Life cycle theory of leadership. Training & Development Journal, 23(5), 26-34.

153 Goleman, D. (1998). Working with emotional intelligence. Bantam Books.

153 Heslin, P. A., Vandewalle, D., & Latham, G. P. (2006). Keen to help? Managers' implicit person theories and their subsequent employee coaching. Personnel Psychology, 59(4), 871-902. https://doi.org/10.1111/j.1744-6570.2006.00057.x

154 Lally, P., Van Jaarsveld, C. H. M., Potts, H. W. W., & Wardle, J. (2010). How are habits formed: Modelling habit formation in the real world. European Journal of Social Psychology, 40(6), 998-1009. https://doi.org/10.1002/ejsp.674

156 Edmondson, A. C. (1999). Psychological safety and learning behavior in work teams. Administrative Science Quarterly, 44(2), 350-383.

156 Rozovsky, J. (2015, November 17). The five keys to a successful Google team. re:Work. https://rework.withgoogle.com/blog/five-keys-to-a-successful-google-team/

158 Keller, T., & Alsdorf, K. L. (2012). Every good endeavor: Connecting your work to God's work. Dutton.

Chapter 9 What Is Preventing Leaders from Creating Happiness?

162 Gallup. (2022). State of the global workplace: 2022 report. Gallup Press.

164 Drucker, P. F. (1954). The practice of management. Harper & Row.

166 Gallup. (2022). State of the global workplace: 2022 report. Gallup Press.

169 Kerr, S. (1995). On the folly of rewarding A, while hoping for B. Academy of Management Executive, 9(1), 7-14. https://doi.org/10.5465/ame.1995.9503133142

169 Harter, J. K., Schmidt, F. L., Agrawal, S., Plowman, S. K., & Blue, A. (2020). The relationship between engagement at work and organizational outcomes: 2020 Q12 meta-analysis: 10th edition. Gallup.

169 Edmondson, A. C. (1999). Psychological safety and learning behavior in work teams. Administrative Science Quarterly, 44(2), 350-383.

172 Mattingly, V., & Kraiger, K. (2019). Can emotional intelligence be trained? A meta-analytic investigation. Human Resource Management Review, 29(2), 140-155. https://doi.org/10.1016/j.hrmr.2018.03.002

173 Barling, J., & Cloutier, A. (2017). Leaders' mental health at work: Empirical, methodological, and policy directions. Journal of Occupational Health Psychology, 22(3), 394-406. https://doi.org/10.1037/ocp0000055

173 Harms, P. D., Credé, M., Tynan, M., Leon, M., & Jeung, W. (2017). Leadership and stress: A meta-analytic review. The Leadership Quarterly, 28(1), 178-194. https://doi.org/10.1016/j.leaqua.2016.10.006

175 Haar, J. M., Russo, M., Suñe, A., & Ollier-Malaterre, A. (2014). Outcomes of work-life balance on job satisfaction, life satisfaction and mental health: A study across seven cultures. Journal of Vocational Behavior, 85(3), 361-373. https://doi.org/10.1016/j.jvb.2014.08.010

175 Fritz, C., & Sonnentag, S. (2006). Recovery, well-being, and performance-related outcomes: The role of workload and vacation experiences. Journal of Applied Psychology, 91(4), 936-945. https://doi.org/10.1037/0021-9010.91.4.936

Chapter 10 The Ripple Effect of Happiness at Work

182 Harvey, S. B., Modini, M., Joyce, S., Milligan-Saville, J. S., Tan, L., Mykletun, A., Bryant, R. A., Christensen, H., & Mitchell, P. B. (2017). Can work make you mentally ill? A systematic meta-review of work-related risk factors for common mental health problems. Occupational and Environmental Medicine, 74(4), 301–310. https://doi.org/10.1136/oemed-2016-104015

182 Warr, P. (2007). Work, happiness, and unhappiness. Lawrence Erlbaum Associates.

182 Gallup, Inc. (2023). How to improve employee engagement in the workplace. https://www.gallup.com/workplace/285674/improve-employee-engagement-workplace.aspx

182 Harvey, S. B., Modini, M., Joyce, S., Milligan-Saville, J. S., Tan, L., Mykletun, A., Bryant, R. A., Christensen, H., & Mitchell, P. B. (2017). Can work make you mentally ill? Occupational and Environmental Medicine, 74(4), 301–310. https://doi.org/10.1136/oemed-2016-104015

183 Warr, P. (2007). Work, happiness, and unhappiness. Lawrence Erlbaum Associates.

183 World Health Organization. (2022). Mental health at work. World Health Organization. https://www.who.int/teams/mental-health-and-substance-use/promotion-prevention/mental-health-at-work

183 Harvey, S. B., Modini, M., Joyce, S., Milligan-Saville, J. S., Tan, L., Mykletun, A., Bryant, R. A., Christensen, H., & Mitchell, P. B. (2017). Can work make you mentally ill? Occupational and Environmental Medicine, 74(4), 301–310. https://doi.org/10.1136/oemed-2016-104015

184 McEwen, B. S. (2007). Physiology and neurobiology of stress and adaptation: Central role of the brain. Physiological Reviews, 87(3), 873–904. https://doi.org/10.1152/physrev.00041.2006

184 Cohen, S., Janicki-Deverts, D., & Miller, G. E. (2012). Psychological stress and disease. *JAMA, 298*(14), 1685–1687. https://doi.org/10.1001/jama.298.14.1685

184 American Institute of Stress. (2022). *What is the true cost of work-related stress?* https://www.stress.org/news/what-is-the-true-cost-of-work-related-stress/

184 Epel, E. S., Blackburn, E. H., Lin, J., Dhabhar, F. S., Adler, N. E., Morrow, J. D., & Cawthon, R. M. (2004). Accelerated telomere shortening in response to life stress. Proceedings of the National Academy of Sciences, 101(49), 17312–17315. https://doi.org/10.1073/pnas.0407162101

184 Puterman, E., Weiss, J., Lin, J., Schilf, S., Slusher, A. L., Johansen, K. L., ... & Epel, E. S. (2016). Predictors of cellular aging in older adults. Brain, Behavior, and Immunity, 54, 1–9. https://doi.org/10.1016/j.bbi.2015.12.002

185 Dewa, C. S., Loong, D., Bonato, S., & Hees, H. (2014). Incidence rates of sickness absence related to mental disorders: A systematic literature review. BMC Public Health, 14, Article 205. https://doi.org/10.1186/1471-2458-14-205

185 Goetzel, R. Z., Roemer, E. C., Liss-Levinson, R. C., & Samoly, D. K. (2018). Workplace health promotion: Policy recommendations that encourage employers to support health improvement programs for their workers. Health Affairs, 37(11), 1823–1831. https://doi.org/10.1377/hlthaff.2018.05431

185 American Institute of Stress. (2022). What is the true cost of work-related stress? https://www.stress.org/news/what-is-the-true-cost-of-work-related-stress/

185 Goh, J., Pfeffer, J., & Zenios, S. A. (2016). The relationship between workplace stressors and mortality and health costs in the United States. Management Science, 62(2), 608–628. https://doi.org/10.1287/mnsc.2014.2115

186 Pew Research Center. (2021). Where Americans find meaning in life. Pew Research Center Report.

186 Steger, M. F., Dik, B. J., & Duffy, R. D. (2012). Measuring meaningful work: The Work and Meaning Inventory (WAMI). Journal of Career Assessment, 20(3), 322–337. https://doi.org/10.1177/1069072711436160

186 Wrzesniewski, A., McCauley, C., Rozin, P., & Schwartz, B. (1997). Jobs, careers, and callings: People's relations to their work. Journal of Research in Personality, 31(1), 21–33. https://doi.org/10.1006/jrpe.1997.2162

187 Greenhaus, J. H., & Beutell, N. J. (1985). Sources of conflict between work and family roles. Academy of Management Review, 10(1), 76–88. https://doi.org/10.5465/amr.1985.4277352

187 Frone, M. R. (2003). Work–family balance. In J. C. Quick & L. E. Tetrick (Eds.), Handbook of occupational health psychology (pp. 143–162). American Psychological Association. https://doi.org/10.1037/10474-007

188 Voydanoff, P. (2004). The effects of work demands and resources on work-to-family conflict and facilitation. Journal of Marriage and Family, 66(2), 398–412. https://doi.org/10.1111/j.1741-3737.2004.00028.x

188 Frone, M. R. (2003). Work–family balance. In J. C. Quick & L. E. Tetrick (Eds.), Handbook of occupational health psychology (pp. 143–

227

162). American Psychological Association.
https://doi.org/10.1037/10474-007

188 Amstad, F. T., Meier, L. L., Fasel, U., Elfering, A., & Semmer, N.
K. (2011). A meta-analysis of work–family conflict and various
outcomes. Journal of Occupational Health Psychology, 16(2), 151–169.
https://doi.org/10.1037/a0022170

188 Crouter, A. C., Bumpus, M. F., Head, M. R., & McHale, S. M.
(2001). Implications of overwork and overload for the quality of men's
family relationships. Journal of Marriage and Family, 63(2), 404–416.
https://doi.org/10.1111/j.1741-3737.2001.00404.x

189 Voydanoff, P. (2004). The effects of work demands and resources
on work-to-family conflict and facilitation. Journal of Marriage and
Family, 66(2), 398–412. https://doi.org/10.1111/j.1741-
3737.2004.00028.x

189 Greenhaus, J. H., & Beutell, N. J. (1985). Sources of conflict
between work and family roles. Academy of Management Review, 10(1),
76–88. https://doi.org/10.5465/amr.1985.4277352

189 Crouter, A. C., Bumpus, M. F., Head, M. R., & McHale, S. M.
(2001). Implications of overwork and overload for the quality of men's
family relationships. Journal of Marriage and Family, 63(2), 404–416.
https://doi.org/10.1111/j.1741-3737.2001.00404.x

190 Johnson, M. K., & Mortimer, J. T. (2011). Origins and outcomes of
judgments about work. Social Forces, 89(4), 1239-1260.
https://doi.org/10.1093/sf/89.4.1239

191 Lyubomirsky, S., King, L., & Diener, E. (2005). The benefits of
frequent positive affect: Does happiness lead to success? Psychological
Bulletin, 131(6), 803-855. https://doi.org/10.1037/0033-2909.131.6.803

191 Judge, T. A., Thoresen, C. J., Bono, J. E., & Patton, G. K. (2001).
The job satisfaction-job performance relationship: A qualitative and
quantitative review. Psychological Bulletin, 127(3), 376-407.
https://doi.org/10.1037/0033-2909.127.3.376

192 De Witte, H., Pienaar, J., & De Cuyper, N. (2016). Review of 30 years of longitudinal studies on the association between job insecurity and health and well-being: Is there causal evidence? Australian Psychologist, 51(1), 18-31. https://doi.org/10.1111/ap.12176

192 Chetty, R., Hendren, N., Kline, P., & Saez, E. (2014). Where is the land of opportunity? The geography of intergenerational mobility in the United States. The Quarterly Journal of Economics, 129(4), 1553-1623. https://doi.org/10.1093/qje/qju022

192 Sonnentag, S., Mojza, E. J., Binnewies, C., & Scholl, A. (2008). Being engaged at work and detached at home: A week-level study on work engagement, psychological detachment, and affect. Work & Stress, 22(3), 257-276. https://doi.org/10.1080/02678370802379440

192 Rodell, J. B. (2013). Finding meaning through volunteering: Why do employees volunteer and what does it mean for their jobs? Academy of Management Journal, 56(5), 1274-1294. https://doi.org/10.5465/amj.2012.0611

193 Brand, J. E. (2015). The far-reaching impact of job loss and unemployment. Annual Review of Sociology, 41, 359-375. https://doi.org/10.1146/annurev-soc-071913-043237

193 Ten Brummelhuis, L. L., & Bakker, A. B. (2012). A resource perspective on the work-home interface: The work-home resources model. American Psychologist, 67(7), 545-556. https://doi.org/10.1037/a0027974

193 Ilies, R., Schwind, K. M., Wagner, D. T., Johnson, M. D., DeRue, D. S., & Ilgen, D. R. (2007). When can employees have a family life? The effects of daily workload and affect on work-family conflict and social behaviors at home. Journal of Applied Psychology, 92(5), 1368-1379. https://doi.org/10.1037/0021-9010.92.5.1368

194 Putnam, R. D. (2000). Bowling alone: The collapse and revival of American community. Simon & Schuster.

195 Goh, J., Pfeffer, J., & Zenios, S. A. (2016). The relationship between workplace stressors and mortality and health costs in the United States. Management Science, 62(2), 608-628. https://doi.org/10.1287/mnsc.2014.2115

197 Harter, J. K., Schmidt, F. L., Agrawal, S., Plowman, S. K., & Blue, A. (2020). The relationship between engagement at work and organizational outcomes: 2020 Q12 meta-analysis: 10th edition. Gallup.

200 Harter, J. K., Schmidt, F. L., Agrawal, S., Plowman, S. K., & Blue, A. (2020). The relationship between engagement at work and organizational outcomes: 2020 Q12 meta-analysis: 10th edition. Gallup.

200 Ten Brummelhuis, L. L., & Bakker, A. B. (2012). A resource perspective on the work-home interface: The work-home resources model. American Psychologist, 67(7), 545-556. https://doi.org/10.1037/a0027974

Special Note: Gallup offers a current State of the Global Workplace report at https://www.gallup.com/workplace/349484/state-of-the-global-workplace.aspx

INDEX

A
absenteeism, 7, 39, 41, 134-136, 138, 141
accountability, 18, 77, 94, 96, 98, 101, 126, 149, 151, 153, 157, 166
Achor, S. (2010), 32, 43, 44, 46, 91
ActivTrak (2024), 133
Allen et al. (2010), 25, 42
Allen, J. (2020), 28
Amabile & Kramer (2011), 121
American Institute of Stress (2022), 135, 184, 185
American Institute of Stress (2024), 134
Amstad et al. (2011), 188
appreciation, 20, 67, 107, 124, 148, 150, 152
autonomy, 24, 88, 89, 175
Avolio & Gardner (2005), 125

B
BBailey et al. (2017), 25
Bakker & Demerouti (2008), 72
Bakker & Demerouti (2017), 33
Bakker et al. (2014), 25, 26
Barling & Cloutier (2017), 173
Barsade & Gibson (2012), 26, 104, 120
Baumeister & Leary (1995), 123
benefits, 38, 44, 54, 58, 63, 66, 70, 72, 75, 159, 184, 192, 194, 198, 199
Bordia et al. (2004), 112
Boushey & Glynn (2012), 131
Brand (2015), 193
Breevaart et al. (2014), 118
Brotman & Sack (2025), 109

Buffini & Company (2024), 115
Burbano (2016), 54
burnout, 24, 134, 136, 138, 171-173, 182
Business Roundtable (2019), 77

C
Cameron (2012), 75
career development, 190
Chetty et al. (2014), 192
Chi et al. (2011), 120
Clifford (2015), 136
coaching, 92, 93, 98, 118, 170
Cockshaw et al. (2013), 123
Cohen et al. (2012), 184
collaboration, 2, 32, 37, 46, 59, 68, 120
Colquitt et al. (2001), 23
communication, 5, 19-22, 41, 70, 87, 94, 96, 98-100, 108-112, 114, 115, 124, 138, 149, 151, 152, 155, 157, 201
compensation, 15, 54, 55, 70, 73, 77, 85, 98, 136, 137, 164, 166, 177, 184, 186, 191
Covey et al. (2022), 116
creativity, 10, 33, 34, 46, 49, 81, 120, 155
Crouter et al. (2001), 188, 189

D
Daniels (1994), 151
Davis (2009), 35
De Neve et al. (2023), 75
De Witte et al. (2016), 192
Deal et al. (2013), 24
Detert & Burris (2007), 137
Dewa et al. (2014), 185

www.ingramcontent.com/pod-product-compliance
Lightning Source LLC
Chambersburg PA
CBHW071650200326
41519CB00012BA/2465